SECRET RESTAURANT ★RECIPES★

FROM THE EDITORS OF FAVORITE BRAND NAME RECIPES™

pil

Publications International, Ltd.

Pictured on the front cover *(clockwise from top left):* Guacamole Burger *(page 98)*, Strawberry-Topped Pancakes *(page 12)*, Cheddar Biscuits *(page 142)*, The Big Onion *(page 56)*, Coleslaw *(page 150)* and Rich and Gooey Cinnamon Bun *(page 10)*.
Pictured on the back cover *(left to right):* Classic Patty Melt *(page 104)*, Thai Chicken Pizza *(page 122)* and Chocolate Chunk Pizza Cookie *(page 158)*.

TABLE OF CONTENTS

BREAKFAST AND BRUNCH

STRAWBERRY BANANA FRENCH TOAST
MAKES 2 SERVINGS

1 cup sliced fresh strawberries (about 8 medium)

2 teaspoons sugar

2 eggs

½ cup milk

3 tablespoons all-purpose flour

1 teaspoon vanilla

⅛ teaspoon salt

1 tablespoon butter

4 slices (1 inch thick) egg bread or country bread

1 banana, cut into ¼-inch slices

Whipped cream and powdered sugar (optional)

Maple syrup

1 Combine strawberries and sugar in small bowl; toss to coat. Set aside while preparing French toast.

2 Whisk eggs, milk, flour, vanilla and salt in shallow bowl or pie plate until well blended. Melt ½ tablespoon butter in large skillet over medium-high heat. Working with 2 slices at a time, dip bread in egg mixture, turning to coat completely; let excess drip off. Add to skillet; cook 3 to 4 minutes per side or until golden brown. Repeat with remaining butter and bread slices.

3 Top each serving with strawberry mixture and banana slices. Garnish with whipped cream and powdered sugar; serve with maple syrup.

BAKED APPLE PANCAKE

MAKES 2 TO 4 SERVINGS

3 tablespoons butter

3 medium Granny Smith apples (about 1¼ pounds), peeled and cut into ¼-inch slices

½ cup packed dark brown sugar

1½ teaspoons ground cinnamon

½ teaspoon plus pinch of salt, divided

4 eggs

⅓ cup whipping cream

⅓ cup milk

2 tablespoons granulated sugar

½ teaspoon vanilla

⅔ cup all-purpose flour

1 Melt butter in 8-inch ovenproof nonstick or cast iron skillet over medium heat. Add apples, brown sugar, cinnamon and pinch of salt; cook about 8 minutes or until apples begin to soften, stirring occasionally. Spread apples in even layer in skillet; set aside to cool 30 minutes.

2 After apples have cooled 30 minutes, preheat oven to 425°F. Whisk eggs in large bowl until foamy. Add cream, milk, granulated sugar, vanilla and remaining ½ teaspoon salt; whisk until blended. Sift flour into egg mixture; whisk until batter is well blended and smooth. Set aside 15 minutes.

3 Stir batter; pour evenly over apple mixture. Place skillet on rimmed baking sheet in case of drips (or place baking sheet or piece of foil in oven beneath skillet).

4 Bake about 16 minutes or until top is golden brown and pancake is loose around edge. Cool 1 minute; loosen edge of pancake with spatula, if necessary. Place large serving plate or cutting board on top of skillet and invert pancake onto plate. Serve warm.

PECAN WAFFLES

MAKES 8 WAFFLES

2¼ cups all-purpose flour

3 tablespoons sugar

1 tablespoon baking powder

½ teaspoon salt

2 cups milk

2 eggs, beaten

¼ cup vegetable oil

¾ cup chopped pecans, toasted*

Butter and maple syrup for serving

To toast pecans, cook in medium skillet over medium heat 2 minutes or until lightly browned, stirring frequently.

1 Preheat classic round waffle iron; grease lightly.

2 Whisk flour, sugar, baking powder and salt in large bowl. Whisk milk, eggs and oil in medium bowl. Add to flour mixture; stir just until blended. Stir in pecans.

3 For each waffle, pour about ½ cup batter into waffle iron. Close lid and bake until steaming stops. Serve with butter and maple syrup.

RICH AND GOOEY CINNAMON BUNS
MAKES 12 BUNS

DOUGH

- 1 package (¼ ounce) active dry yeast
- 1 cup warm milk (105° to 115°F)
- 2 eggs, beaten
- ½ cup granulated sugar
- ¼ cup (½ stick) butter, softened
- 1 teaspoon salt
- 4 to 4¼ cups all-purpose flour

FILLING

- 1 cup packed brown sugar
- 3 tablespoons ground cinnamon
  Pinch of salt
- 6 tablespoons (¾ stick) butter, softened

ICING

- 1½ cups powdered sugar
- 3 ounces cream cheese, softened
- ¼ cup (½ stick) butter, softened
- ½ teaspoon vanilla
- ⅛ teaspoon salt

1 Dissolve yeast in warm milk in large bowl of electric mixer. Add eggs, granulated sugar, ¼ cup butter and 1 teaspoon salt; beat at medium speed until well blended. Add 4 cups flour; beat at low speed until dough begins to come together. Knead with dough hook at low speed about 5 minutes or until smooth, elastic and slightly sticky, adding additional flour, 1 tablespoon at a time, if necessary to prevent sticking.

2 Shape dough into a ball. Place in large greased bowl; turn to grease top. Cover and let rise in warm place about 1 hour or until doubled in size. Meanwhile, for filling, combine brown sugar, cinnamon and pinch of salt in small bowl; mix well.

3 Spray 13×9-inch baking pan with nonstick cooking spray. Roll out dough into 18×14-inch rectangle on floured surface. Spread 6 tablespoons butter evenly over dough; top with cinnamon-sugar mixture. Beginning with long side, roll up dough tightly jelly-roll style; pinch seam to seal. Cut log crosswise into 12 slices; place slices cut sides up in prepared pan. Cover and let rise in warm place about 30 minutes or until almost doubled in size. Preheat oven to 350°F.

4 Bake 20 to 25 minutes or until golden brown. Meanwhile, for icing, combine powdered sugar, cream cheese, ¼ cup butter, vanilla and ⅛ teaspoon salt in medium bowl; beat with electric mixer at medium speed 2 minutes or until smooth and creamy. Spread icing generously over warm cinnamon buns.

STRAWBERRY-TOPPED PANCAKES

MAKES 2 SERVINGS (6 LARGE PANCAKES)

1½ cups sliced fresh strawberries

2 tablespoons seedless strawberry jam

1¼ cups all-purpose flour

¼ cup sugar

1 teaspoon baking powder

1 teaspoon baking soda

¼ teaspoon salt

1¼ cups buttermilk

1 egg, lightly beaten

1 to 2 tablespoons vegetable oil

Whipped cream (optional)

1 Combine strawberries and strawberry jam in medium bowl; stir gently to coat. Set aside while preparing pancakes.

2 Combine flour, sugar, baking powder, baking soda and salt in large bowl; mix well. Add buttermilk and egg; whisk until blended.

3 Heat 1 tablespoon oil in large skillet over medium heat or brush griddle with oil. For each pancake, pour ½ cup of batter into skillet, spreading into 5- to 6-inch circle. Cook 3 to 4 minutes or until bottom is golden brown and small bubbles appear on surface. Turn pancake; cook about 2 minutes or until golden brown. Add additional oil to skillet as needed.

4 For each serving, stack 3 pancakes; top with strawberry mixture. Garnish with whipped cream.

BEVERAGES

PUMPKIN SPICE LATTE
MAKES 2 SERVINGS

1¾ cups milk, divided

½ cup canned pumpkin

3 tablespoons packed brown sugar

1 teaspoon grated fresh ginger

1 teaspoon pumpkin pie spice

½ teaspoon ground cinnamon, plus additional for garnish

¼ teaspoon salt

⅛ teaspoon coarsely ground black pepper

1 cup strong-brewed hot coffee*

1 tablespoon vanilla

Whipped cream (optional)

*Use about 1 tablespoon ground espresso roast or other dark roast coffee for each 3 ounces of water.

1 Combine ½ cup milk, pumpkin, brown sugar, ginger, pumpkin pie spice, ½ teaspoon cinnamon, salt and pepper in medium saucepan; whisk until well blended. Cook over medium-low heat 10 minutes, whisking frequently. Remove from heat; whisk in coffee and vanilla. Strain through fine-mesh strainer into medium bowl.

2 Bring remaining 1¼ cups milk to a simmer in small saucepan over medium-high heat. For froth, whisk vigorously 30 seconds. Whisk into espresso mixture until blended. Garnish with whipped cream and additional cinnamon.

CHOCOLATE FROSTY >

MAKES 2 SERVINGS

¼ cup unsweetened cocoa powder

2 cups milk, divided

½ cup sweetened condensed milk

1 tablespoon corn syrup

1 teaspoon vanilla

1 Whisk cocoa and ¼ cup milk in large measuring cup with pour spout until well blended. Whisk in 1½ cups milk, sweetened condensed milk, corn syrup and vanilla. Pour mixture into ice cube tray. Freeze 4 hours or until firm.

2 Loosen frozen chocolate cubes with thin knife; remove from ice cube trays. Place in blender with remaining ¼ cup milk; pulse to break up chunks. Blend about 30 seconds or until smooth.

PEACH ICED TEA

MAKES 4 SERVINGS

4 cups water

3 black tea bags

¼ cup sugar

1 can (about 11 ounces) peach nectar

1 cup frozen peach slices

Ice cubes

1 Bring water to a boil in medium saucepan over high heat. Remove from heat; add tea bags and let steep 5 minutes. Remove tea bags; stir in sugar until dissolved. Cool to room temperature.

2 Stir in peach nectar and peach slices. Refrigerate until cold. Serve over ice.

ORANGE WHIP >

MAKES 2 SERVINGS

2 cups ice cubes

1 can (12 ounces) frozen orange juice concentrate with pulp, partially thawed

1 cup milk

¼ cup powdered sugar

½ teaspoon vanilla

Combine ice, orange juice concentrate, milk, powdered sugar and vanilla in blender; pulse to break up ice. Blend until smooth.

FROSTED LEMONADE

MAKES 3 SERVINGS

½ cup sugar

3 cups water, divided

1 cup lemon juice

6 cups vanilla ice cream

1 Combine sugar and ½ cup water in small saucepan; cook over medium-high heat until sugar is dissolved and mixture is clear. Remove from heat; cool slightly.

2 Combine lemon juice, remaining 2½ cups water and sugar syrup in pitcher or large measuring cup. Refrigerate until cold.

3 For each serving, combine 1 cup lemonade and 2 cups ice cream in blender; blend until smooth.

FROZEN MUDSLIDE >

MAKES 1 SERVING

1 cup vanilla ice cream

1 ounce vodka

1 ounce coffee liqueur

1 ounce Irish cream liqueur

1 to 2 tablespoons whipping cream or half-and-half (optional)

Chocolate syrup (optional)

Whipped cream and mini chocolate chips (optional)

1 Combine ice cream, vodka, coffee liqueur and Irish cream liqueur in blender; blend until smooth. Add cream, if desired, to reach desired consistency.

2 If desired, garnish glass with chocolate syrup before pouring drink into glass. Hold glass at 90-degree angle; gently squeeze chocolate syrup onto side of glass while turning glass. Or squeeze syrup in vertical squiggles up and down side of glass.

3 Pour drink into prepared glass; garnish with whipped cream and chocolate chips.

CHERRY LIMEADE

MAKES 1 SERVING

Crushed ice

¼ lime

1 can (12 ounces) lemon-lime soda

2 tablespoons thawed frozen limeade concentrate

2 tablespoons liquid from maraschino cherry jar

1 maraschino cherry

Fill tall glass with crushed ice. Squeeze lime wedge over ice and drop lime into glass. Pour soda, limeade and cherry liquid into glass; stir gently. Garnish with maraschino cherry.

STRAWBERRY LEMONADE >

MAKES 5 SERVINGS

1 cup sugar

3 cups water, divided

1 cup frozen strawberries

1½ cups lemon juice

1 Combine sugar, 1 cup water and strawberries in small saucepan; bring to a boil over high heat. Boil 5 minutes. Remove from heat; cool completely.

2 Pour strawberry mixture into blender; blend until smooth. Strain into pitcher. Stir in lemon juice and remaining 2 cups water until blended. Refrigerate until cold.

INSPIRED BY APPLEBEE'S® GRILL & BAR

WHITE PEACH SANGRIA

MAKES 8 TO 10 SERVINGS

2 oranges, cut into ¼-inch slices

2 lemons, cut into ¼-inch slices

½ cup sugar

2 bottles (750 milliliters each) dry, fruity white wine (such as Pinot Grigio), chilled

½ cup peach schnapps

3 ripe peaches, pitted and cut into wedges

2 cups ice cubes (about 16 cubes)

1 Place orange and lemon slices in large punch bowl. Pour sugar over fruit; mash lightly until sugar dissolves and fruit begins to break down.

2 Stir in wine, peach schnapps and peaches; mix well. Refrigerate at least 2 hours or up to 10 hours. Add ice cubes just before serving.

COFFEE FRAPPUCCINO >

MAKES 1 SERVING

½ cup ground coffee (preferably dark roast)

1 cup water

½ cup milk

¼ cup sweetened condensed milk

2 tablespoons instant vanilla pudding and pie filling mix

1 tablespoon maple syrup

1 cup ice cubes (about 6)

Whipped cream and unsweetened cocoa powder

1 Brew strong coffee using ground coffee and water.* (You should get about ½ cup coffee. Only half is needed for recipe; reserve remaining half for another use.) Refrigerate until cold.

2 Combine ¼ cup coffee, milk, sweetened condensed milk, pudding mix, maple syrup and ice in blender; blend until smooth. Garnish with whipped cream and cocoa.

* This drink requires very strong coffee. Instead of brewing a small amount, you can substitute 2 tablespoons instant coffee blended with 2 tablespoons hot water or just enough water to dissolve the coffee. Proceed with step 2 as directed.

SHAMROCK SHAKE

MAKES 1 SERVING

2 cups low-fat French vanilla ice cream

½ cup milk, divided

⅛ teaspoon peppermint extract

10 drops green food coloring

Whipped cream and maraschino cherry (optional)

Combine ice cream, ¼ cup milk, peppermint extract and green food coloring in blender; blend until smooth. Add additional ¼ cup milk if needed to reach desired consistency. Garnish with whipped cream and cherry.

CHOCOLATE CAKE MILKSHAKE

MAKES 1 SERVING

1 slice (⅛ of cake) Rich Chocolate
  Cake (recipe follows)

½ cup milk

2 scoops vanilla ice cream
  (about 1 cup total)

1 Prepare and frost Rich Chocolate Cake.

2 Combine milk, ice cream and cake slice in blender; blend just until cake is incorporated but texture of shake is not completely smooth.

RICH CHOCOLATE CAKE

MAKES 8 TO 10 SERVINGS

1 package (about 15 ounces)
  devil's food cake mix

1 cup cold water

1 cup mayonnaise

3 eggs

1½ containers (16 ounces each)
  chocolate frosting

1 Preheat oven to 350°F. Spray 2 (9-inch) round cake pans with nonstick cooking spray.

2 Beat cake mix, water, mayonnaise and eggs in large bowl with electric mixer at low speed 30 seconds. Beat at medium speed 2 minutes. Pour into prepared pans.

3 Bake about 25 minutes or until toothpick inserted into centers comes out clean. Cool in pans 10 minutes; remove to wire racks to cool completely.

4 Fill and frost cake with chocolate frosting.

APPETIZERS

MOZZARELLA STICKS
MAKES 4 TO 6 SERVINGS

¼ cup all-purpose flour

2 eggs

1 tablespoon water

1 cup dry bread crumbs

2 teaspoons Italian seasoning

½ teaspoon salt

½ teaspoon garlic powder

1 package (12 ounces) string cheese (12 sticks)

Vegetable oil for frying

1 cup marinara or pizza sauce, heated

1 Place flour in shallow bowl. Whisk eggs and water in another shallow bowl. Combine bread crumbs, Italian seasoning, salt and garlic powder in third shallow bowl.

2 Coat each piece of cheese with flour. Dip in egg mixture, letting excess drip back into bowl. Roll in bread crumb mixture to coat. Dip again in egg mixture and roll again in bread crumb mixture. Refrigerate until ready to cook.

3 Heat 2 inches of oil in large saucepan over medium-high heat to 350°F; adjust heat to maintain temperature. Add cheese sticks; cook about 1 minute or until golden brown. Drain on wire rack. Serve with sauce for dipping.

BUFFALO WINGS

MAKES 4 SERVINGS

1 cup hot pepper sauce

⅓ cup vegetable oil, plus additional for frying

1 teaspoon sugar

½ teaspoon ground red pepper

½ teaspoon garlic powder

½ teaspoon Worcestershire sauce

⅛ teaspoon black pepper

1 pound chicken wings, tips discarded, separated at joints

Blue cheese or ranch dressing

Celery sticks (optional)

1 Combine hot pepper sauce, ⅓ cup oil, sugar, red pepper, garlic powder, Worcestershire sauce and black pepper in small saucepan; cook over medium heat 20 minutes. Remove from heat; pour sauce into large bowl.

2 Heat 3 inches of oil in large saucepan over medium-high heat to 350°F; adjust heat to maintain temperature. Add wings; cook 10 minutes or until crispy. Drain on wire rack set over paper towels.

3 Transfer wings to bowl of sauce; stir to coat. Serve with blue cheese dressing and celery sticks, if desired.

SPINACH-ARTICHOKE DIP

MAKES 6 TO 8 SERVINGS

1 package (8 ounces) baby spinach

1 package (8 ounces) cream cheese, softened

¼ cup mayonnaise

1 clove garlic, minced

1 teaspoon dried basil

½ teaspoon dried thyme

¼ teaspoon salt

¼ teaspoon red pepper flakes

¼ teaspoon black pepper

1 can (about 14 ounces) artichoke hearts, drained and chopped

¾ cup grated Parmesan cheese, divided

Toasted French bread slices or tortilla chips

1 Preheat oven to 350°F. Spray 8-inch oval, round or square baking dish with nonstick cooking spray.

2 Place spinach in large microwavable bowl; cover and microwave 2 minutes or until wilted. Uncover; let stand until cool enough to handle. Squeeze dry and coarsely chop.

3 Whisk cream cheese, mayonnaise, garlic, basil, thyme, salt, red pepper flakes and black pepper in medium bowl until well blended. Stir in spinach, artichokes and ½ cup cheese. Spread in prepared baking dish; sprinkle with remaining ¼ cup cheese.

4 Bake about 30 minutes or until edges are golden brown. Cool slightly; serve warm with toasted bread slices.

POTATO SKINS
MAKES 6 TO 8 SERVINGS

8 medium baking potatoes
(6 to 8 ounces each)

1 tablespoon vegetable oil

1 teaspoon salt

⅛ teaspoon black pepper

1 tablespoon butter, melted

1 cup (4 ounces) shredded
Cheddar cheese

8 slices bacon, crisp-cooked
and coarsely chopped

1 cup sour cream

3 tablespoons snipped fresh chives

1 Preheat oven to 400°F.

2 Prick potatoes all over with fork. Rub oil over potatoes; sprinkle with salt and pepper. Place in 13×9-inch baking pan. Bake 1 hour or until fork-tender. Let stand until cool enough to handle. *Reduce oven temperature to 350°F.*

3 Cut potatoes in half lengthwise; cut small slice off bottom of each half so potato halves will lay flat. Scoop out soft middles of potato skins; reserve for another use. Place potato halves skin sides up in baking pan; brush with butter.

4 Bake 20 to 25 minutes or until crisp. Turn potatoes over; top with cheese and bacon. Bake 5 minutes or until cheese is melted. Cool slightly. Top with sour cream and chives just before serving.

CHICKEN FAJITA NACHOS

MAKES 4 SERVINGS

2 tablespoons vegetable oil, divided

2 red bell peppers, cut into thin strips

1 large onion, halved and thinly sliced

2 tablespoons fajita seasoning mix (from 1¼-ounce package), divided

2 tablespoons water, divided

1 large boneless skinless chicken breast (about 12 ounces), cut into 2×1-inch strips

4 cups tortilla chips (about 30 chips)

½ cup (2 ounces) shredded Cheddar cheese

½ cup (2 ounces) shredded Monterey Jack cheese

1 jalapeño pepper, seeded and thinly sliced

1 cup shredded lettuce

½ cup salsa, plus additional for serving

Sour cream and guacamole (optional)

1 Heat 1 tablespoon oil in large skillet over medium-high heat. Add bell peppers and onion; cook 5 minutes or until tender and browned in spots, stirring frequently. Transfer to large bowl; stir in 1 tablespoon fajita seasoning mix and 1 tablespoon water.

2 Heat remaining 1 tablespoon oil in same skillet over medium-high heat. Add chicken; cook 7 to 10 minutes or until cooked through, stirring occasionally. Add remaining 1 tablespoon fajita seasoning mix and 1 tablespoon water; cook and stir until chicken is coated.

3 Preheat broiler. Place chips in 11×7-inch baking dish or pan; top with vegetables, chicken, Cheddar and Monterey Jack cheeses and jalapeño.

4 Broil 2 to 4 minutes or until cheeses are melted. Top with lettuce, ½ cup salsa, sour cream and guacamole, if desired. Serve immediately.

TOASTED RAVIOLI

MAKES 20 TO 24 RAVIOLI

1 cup all-purpose flour

2 eggs

¼ cup water

1 cup plain dry bread crumbs

1 teaspoon Italian seasoning

¾ teaspoon garlic powder

¼ teaspoon salt

½ cup grated Parmesan cheese

2 tablespoons finely chopped fresh parsley (optional)

Vegetable oil for frying

1 package (12 to 16 ounces) meat or cheese ravioli, thawed if frozen

Pasta sauce, heated

1 Place flour in shallow bowl. Whisk eggs and water in another shallow bowl. Combine bread crumbs, Italian seasoning, garlic powder and salt in third shallow bowl. Combine cheese and parsley, if desired, in large bowl.

2 Heat 2 inches of oil in large deep skillet over medium-high heat to 350°F; adjust heat to maintain temperature.

3 Coat ravioli with flour. Dip in egg mixture, letting excess drip back into bowl. Roll in bread crumb mixture to coat. Working in batches, carefully add ravioli to hot oil; cook about 1 minute or until golden brown, turning once. Remove from oil with slotted spoon; drain on paper towel-lined plate. Add to bowl with cheese; toss to coat. Serve warm with sauce.

GUACAMOLE

MAKES 2 CUPS

2 large ripe avocados

2 teaspoons lime juice

¼ cup finely chopped red onion

2 tablespoons chopped
   fresh cilantro

½ jalapeño pepper, finely chopped

½ teaspoon salt

1 Place avocados in large bowl; sprinkle with lime juice and toss to coat. Mash to desired consistency with fork or potato masher.

2 Add onion, cilantro, jalapeño and salt; stir gently until well blended. Taste and add additional salt, if desired.

AVOCADO EGG ROLLS

MAKES 8 TO 10 SERVINGS (20 PIECES) AND 1 CUP SAUCE

DIPPING SAUCE

- ½ cup cashew pieces
- ½ cup packed fresh cilantro
- ¼ cup honey
- 2 green onions, coarsely chopped
- 2 cloves garlic
- 1 tablespoon white vinegar
- 1 teaspoon balsamic vinegar
- 1 teaspoon ground cumin
- ½ teaspoon tamarind paste
- ⅛ teaspoon ground turmeric
- ¼ cup olive oil

EGG ROLLS

- 2 medium avocados
- ¼ cup chopped drained oil-packed sun-dried tomatoes
- 2 tablespoons diced red onion
- 2 tablespoons chopped fresh cilantro
- 1 tablespoon lime juice
- ¼ teaspoon salt
- 10 egg roll wrappers
- Vegetable oil for frying

1 For sauce, combine cashews, cilantro, honey, green onions, garlic, white vinegar, balsamic vinegar, cumin, tamarind paste and turmeric in food processor; process until coarsely chopped. With motor running, drizzle in olive oil in thin steady stream; process until finely chopped and well blended. Refrigerate until ready to use.

2 For egg rolls, place avocados in medium bowl; coarsely mash with potato masher. Stir in sundried tomatoes, red onion, chopped cilantro, lime juice and salt until well blended.

3 Working with one egg roll wrapper at a time, place wrapper on work surface with one corner facing you. Spread 2 tablespoons filling horizontally across wrapper. Fold short sides over filling and fold up bottom corner over filling. Moisten top edges with water; roll up egg roll, pressing to seal. Refrigerate until ready to cook.

4 Heat 2 inches of vegetable oil in large saucepan over medium-high heat to 350°F; adjust heat to maintain temperature. Cook egg rolls in batches about 3 minutes or until golden brown, turning once. Drain on paper towel-lined plate. Cut egg rolls in half diagonally; serve with sauce.

BRUSCHETTA
MAKES 1 CUP (8 SERVINGS)

4 plum tomatoes, seeded and diced

½ cup packed fresh basil leaves, finely chopped

5 tablespoons olive oil, divided

2 cloves garlic, minced

2 teaspoons finely chopped oil-packed sun-dried tomatoes

¼ teaspoon salt

⅛ teaspoon black pepper

16 slices Italian bread

2 tablespoons grated Parmesan cheese

1 Combine fresh tomatoes, basil, 3 tablespoons oil, garlic, sun-dried tomatoes, salt and pepper in large bowl; mix well. Let stand at room temperature 1 hour to blend flavors.

2 Preheat oven to 375°F. Place bread on baking sheet. Brush remaining 2 tablespoons oil over one side of each bread slice; sprinkle with cheese. Bake 6 to 8 minutes or until toasted.

3 Top each bread slice with 1 tablespoon tomato mixture.

GREEN BEAN FRIES

MAKES 4 TO 6 SERVINGS

DIP

- ½ cup mayonnaise
- ¼ cup sour cream
- ¼ cup buttermilk
- ¼ cup minced peeled cucumber
- 1½ teaspoons lemon juice
- 1 clove garlic
- 1 teaspoon wasabi powder
- 1 teaspoon prepared horseradish
- ½ teaspoon dried dill
- ½ teaspoon dried parsley flakes
- ½ teaspoon salt
- ⅛ teaspoon ground red pepper

GREEN BEAN FRIES

- 8 ounces fresh green beans, trimmed
- ½ cup all-purpose flour
- ½ cup cornstarch
- ¾ cup milk
- 1 egg
- 1 cup plain dry bread crumbs
- 1 teaspoon salt
- ½ teaspoon onion powder
- ¼ teaspoon garlic powder
- Vegetable oil for frying

1 For dip, combine mayonnaise, sour cream, buttermilk, cucumber, lemon juice, garlic, wasabi, horseradish, dill, parsley flakes, salt and red pepper in blender; blend until smooth. Refrigerate until ready to use.

2 Bring large saucepan of salted water to a boil. Add green beans; cook 4 minutes or until crisp-tender. Drain and run under cold running water to stop cooking.

3 Combine flour and cornstarch in large bowl. Whisk milk and egg in another large bowl. Combine bread crumbs, salt, onion powder and garlic powder in shallow bowl. Place green beans in flour mixture; toss to coat. Working in batches, coat beans with egg mixture, letting excess drip back into bowl. Roll beans in bread crumb mixture to coat. Place on large baking sheet.

4 Heat 3 inches of oil in large saucepan over medium-high heat to 375°F; adjust heat to maintain temperature. Cook green beans in batches about 1 minute or until golden brown. Drain on paper towel-lined plate. Serve warm with dip.

APPETIZERS

CHICKEN BACON QUESADILLAS

MAKES 4 SERVINGS

4 teaspoons vegetable oil, divided

4 fajita-size tortillas (8-inch)

1 cup (4 ounces) shredded Colby-Jack cheese

2 cups coarsely chopped cooked chicken

4 slices bacon, crisp-cooked and coarsely chopped

½ cup pico de gallo

Salsa, sour cream and guacamole

1 Heat large nonstick skillet over medium heat; brush with 1 teaspoon oil. Place one tortilla in skillet; sprinkle with ¼ cup cheese. Spread ½ cup chicken over half of tortilla; top with one fourth of bacon and 2 tablespoons pico de gallo.

2 Cook 1 to 2 minutes or until cheese is melted and bottom of tortilla is lightly browned. Fold tortilla over filling, pressing with spatula. Transfer to cutting board; cool slightly. Cut into wedges. Repeat with remaining ingredients. Serve with salsa, sour cream and guacamole.

APPETIZERS

SALSA
MAKES 4½ CUPS

1 can (28 ounces) whole Italian plum tomatoes, undrained

2 fresh plum tomatoes, seeded and coarsely chopped

2 tablespoons canned diced mild green chiles

1 tablespoon canned diced jalapeño peppers (optional)

1 tablespoon white vinegar

1 clove garlic, minced

1 teaspoon onion powder

1 teaspoon sugar

1 teaspoon ground cumin

½ teaspoon garlic powder

¼ teaspoon salt

Combine tomatoes with juice, fresh tomatoes, green chiles, jalapeños, if desired, vinegar, garlic, onion powder, sugar, cumin, garlic powder and salt in food processor; process until finely chopped.

SPICY CRISPY SHRIMP

MAKES 4 SERVINGS

½ cup mayonnaise

4 teaspoons Thai chili sauce

1 teaspoon honey

½ teaspoon rice vinegar

¾ cup buttermilk

1 egg

¾ cup all-purpose flour

½ cup panko bread crumbs

1 teaspoon salt

½ teaspoon ground sage

½ teaspoon black pepper

¼ teaspoon onion powder

¼ teaspoon garlic powder

¼ teaspoon dried basil

16 to 20 large raw shrimp, peeled, deveined and patted dry

Vegetable oil for frying

2 green onions, thinly sliced (optional)

1 For sauce, combine mayonnaise, chili sauce, honey and vinegar in small bowl; mix well. Cover and refrigerate until ready to serve.

2 Whisk buttermilk and egg in medium bowl until well blended. Combine flour, panko, salt, sage, pepper, onion powder, garlic powder and basil in separate medium bowl; mix well. Dip each shrimp in buttermilk mixture, then in flour mixture, turning to coat completely. Place breaded shrimp on large plate; refrigerate until oil is hot.

3 Heat 2 inches of oil in large saucepan over medium heat to 350°F; adjust heat to maintain temperature. Cook shrimp, 4 to 6 at a time, 2 to 3 minutes or until golden brown, turning halfway through cooking time. Drain on paper towel-lined plate.

4 Transfer shrimp to large bowl; add sauce and toss gently to coat. Garnish with green onions.

SHANGHAI CHICKEN WINGS

MAKES 4 TO 6 SERVINGS

DIP

- ½ cup ranch dressing
- 2 tablespoons buttermilk
- 1 teaspoon prepared horseradish
- ½ teaspoon wasabi powder

SAUCE

- ¾ cup water
- 1 tablespoon cornstarch
- ¼ cup packed dark brown sugar
- ¼ cup soy sauce
- 3 tablespoons lime juice
- 2 tablespoons minced fresh ginger
- 1 teaspoon minced garlic
- ¼ teaspoon red pepper flakes

CHICKEN

- 2 large boneless skinless chicken breasts (about 2 pounds)
- 1 cup all-purpose flour
- ¼ cup cornstarch
- 2 teaspoons salt
- ¼ teaspoon black pepper
- ¼ teaspoon ground red pepper
- ¼ teaspoon paprika
- 2 eggs
- ½ cup milk
- Vegetable oil for frying

1 For dip, combine ranch dressing, buttermilk, horseradish and wasabi in small bowl; mix well. Refrigerate until ready to use.

2 For sauce, whisk water and cornstarch in medium saucepan until smooth. Add brown sugar, soy sauce, lime juice, ginger, garlic and red pepper flakes; whisk until well blended. Bring to a boil over high heat. Reduce heat to low; simmer 10 minutes or until thickened, stirring occasionally. Transfer to large bowl; set aside to cool.

3 Cut chicken into large pieces (about 2×1 inches). Combine flour, cornstarch, salt, black pepper, ground red pepper and paprika in large bowl. Whisk eggs and milk in shallow bowl. Coat chicken with flour mixture. Dip in egg mixture, letting excess drip back into bowl. Coat again with flour mixture; place on baking sheet.

4 Heat 3 inches of oil in large saucepan over medium-high heat to 375°F; adjust heat to maintain temperature. Cook chicken in batches 3 minutes or until golden brown and cooked through, turning once. Drain on paper towel-lined plate. Add chicken to sauce and stir to coat. Remove chicken to serving plate with slotted spoon; serve with dip.

THE BIG ONION

MAKES 4 TO 6 SERVINGS

DIPPING SAUCE

- ½ cup mayonnaise
- 2 tablespoons horseradish
- 1 tablespoon ketchup
- ¼ teaspoon paprika
- ⅛ teaspoon salt
- ⅛ teaspoon ground red pepper
- ⅛ teaspoon dried oregano

ONION

- 1 large sweet onion (about 1 pound)
- Ice water

- 1 cup milk
- 2 eggs
- 1½ cups all-purpose flour
- 1 tablespoon paprika
- 1½ teaspoons salt
- 1½ teaspoons ground red pepper
- ¾ teaspoon black pepper
- ½ teaspoon onion powder
- ½ teaspoon garlic powder
- ¼ teaspoon ground cumin
- Vegetable oil for frying

1 For sauce, combine mayonnaise, horseradish, ketchup, ¼ teaspoon paprika, ⅛ teaspoon salt, ⅛ teaspoon red pepper and oregano in small bowl; mix well. Cover and refrigerate until ready to serve.

2 Cut about ½ inch off top of onion and peel off papery skin. Place onion cut side down on cutting board. Starting ½ inch from root, use large sharp knife to make one slice down to cutting board. Repeat slicing all the way around onion to make 12 to 16 evenly spaced cuts. Turn onion over; gently separate outer pieces. Place onion in large bowl of ice water; let soak 15 minutes.

3 Meanwhile, whisk milk and eggs in large bowl. Combine flour, 1 tablespoon paprika, 1½ teaspoons salt, 1½ teaspoons red pepper, black pepper, onion powder, garlic powder and cumin in separate large bowl.

4 Drain onion, place in bowl of flour mixture. Cover onion with flour mixture, making sure it gets between slices and coats onion completely. Dip onion in milk mixture, turning to coat. Let excess milk mixture drip back into bowl before returning onion to flour mixture, turning to make sure all sides of onion and space between slices are well coated. Place onion on plate or baking sheet; refrigerate while heating oil.

5 Pour enough oil into large deep saucepan, Dutch oven or deep fryer to completely cover onion. Heat oil over medium-high heat to 350°F; adjust heat to maintain temperature. Use wire skimmer or large slotted spoon to carefully lower onion into oil, cut side down. Cook 3 to 4 minutes or until onion begins to brown. Turn and cook 3 minutes or until golden brown. Drain on paper towel-lined plate; sprinkle with salt. Serve immediately with dipping sauce.

SOUPS

CHICKEN NOODLE SOUP
MAKES 8 SERVINGS

2 tablespoons butter

1 cup chopped onion

1 cup sliced carrots

½ cup diced celery

2 tablespoons vegetable oil

1 pound chicken breast tenderloins

1 pound chicken thigh fillets

4 cups chicken broth, divided

2 cups water

1 tablespoon minced fresh parsley, plus additional for garnish

1½ teaspoons salt

½ teaspoon black pepper

3 cups uncooked egg noodles

1 Melt butter in large saucepan or Dutch oven over medium-low heat. Add onion, carrots and celery; cook 15 minutes or until vegetables are soft, stirring occasionally.

2 Meanwhile, heat oil in large skillet over medium-high heat. Add chicken in single layer; cook about 12 minutes or until lightly browned and cooked through, turning once. Transfer chicken to cutting board. Add 1 cup broth to skillet; cook 1 minute, scraping up browned bits from bottom of skillet. Add broth to vegetables. Stir in remaining 3 cups broth, water, 1 tablespoon parsley, salt and pepper.

3 Chop chicken into bite-size pieces when cool enough to handle. Add to soup; bring to a boil over medium-high heat. Reduce heat to medium-low; cook 15 minutes. Add noodles; cook 15 minutes or until noodles are tender. Ladle into bowls; garnish with additional parsley.

PASTA FAGIOLI

MAKES 8 SERVINGS

2 tablespoons olive oil, divided

1 pound ground beef

1 cup chopped onion

1 cup diced carrots
    (about 2 medium)

1 cup diced celery (about 2 stalks)

3 cloves garlic, minced

4 cups beef broth

1 can (28 ounces) diced tomatoes

1 can (15 ounces) tomato sauce

1 tablespoon cider vinegar

2 teaspoons sugar

1½ teaspoons dried basil

1¼ teaspoons salt

1 teaspoon dried oregano

¾ teaspoon dried thyme

2 cups uncooked ditalini pasta

1 can (about 15 ounces) dark
    red kidney beans, rinsed
    and drained

1 can (about 15 ounces) cannellini
    beans, rinsed and drained

Grated Romano cheese

1 Heat 1 tablespoon oil in large saucepan or Dutch oven over medium-high heat. Add beef; cook 5 minutes or until browned, stirring to break up meat. Transfer to medium bowl; set aside. Drain fat from saucepan.

2 Heat remaining 1 tablespoon oil in same saucepan over medium-high heat. Add onion, carrots and celery; cook and stir 5 minutes or until vegetables are tender. Add garlic; cook and stir 1 minute. Add cooked beef, broth, tomatoes, tomato sauce, vinegar, sugar, basil, salt, oregano and thyme; bring to a boil. Reduce heat to medium-low; cover and simmer 30 minutes.

3 Add pasta, kidney beans and cannellini beans; cook over medium heat 10 minutes or until pasta is tender, stirring frequently. Ladle into bowls; top with cheese.

BROCCOLI CHEESE SOUP
MAKES 6 SERVINGS

6 tablespoons (¾ stick) butter

1 cup chopped onion

1 clove garlic, minced

¼ cup all-purpose flour

2 cups vegetable broth

2 cups milk

1½ teaspoons Dijon mustard

½ teaspoon salt

¼ teaspoon ground nutmeg

¼ teaspoon black pepper

⅛ teaspoon hot pepper sauce

1 package (16 ounces) frozen broccoli (5 cups)

2 carrots, shredded (1 cup)

6 ounces pasteurized process cheese, cubed

1 cup (4 ounces) shredded sharp Cheddar cheese, plus additional for garnish

1 Melt butter in large saucepan or Dutch oven over medium-low heat. Add onion; cook and stir 10 minutes or until softened. Add garlic; cook and stir 1 minute. Increase heat to medium. Whisk in flour until smooth; cook and stir 3 minutes without browning.

2 Gradually whisk in broth and milk. Add mustard, salt, nutmeg, black pepper and hot pepper sauce; cook about 15 minutes or until thickened.

3 Add broccoli; cook 15 minutes. Add carrots; cook 10 minutes or until vegetables are tender.

4 Transfer half of soup to food processor or blender; process until smooth. Return to saucepan. Add process cheese and 1 cup Cheddar; cook and stir over low heat until cheeses are melted. Ladle into bowls; garnish with additional Cheddar.

BLACK BEAN SOUP

MAKES 4 TO 6 SERVINGS

2 tablespoons vegetable oil

1 cup diced onion

1 stalk celery, diced

2 carrots, diced

½ small green bell pepper, diced

4 cloves garlic, minced

4 cans (about 15 ounces each) black beans, rinsed and drained, divided

4 cups (32 ounces) chicken or vegetable broth, divided

2 tablespoons cider vinegar

2 teaspoons chili powder

½ teaspoon salt

½ teaspoon ground red pepper

½ teaspoon ground cumin

¼ teaspoon liquid smoke

Garnishes: sour cream, chopped green onions and shredded Cheddar cheese

1 Heat oil in large saucepan or Dutch oven over medium-low heat. Add onion, celery, carrots, bell pepper and garlic; cook 10 minutes, stirring occasionally.

2 Combine half of beans and 1 cup broth in food processor or blender; process until smooth. Add to vegetables in saucepan.

3 Stir in remaining beans, broth, vinegar, chili powder, salt, red pepper, cumin and liquid smoke; bring to a boil over high heat. Reduce heat to medium-low; cook 1 hour or until vegetables are tender and soup is thickened. Garnish as desired.

HEARTY TUSCAN SOUP

MAKES 6 TO 8 SERVINGS

1 teaspoon olive oil

1 pound bulk mild or hot Italian sausage*

1 medium onion, chopped

3 cloves garlic, minced

¼ cup all-purpose flour

5 cups chicken broth

1 teaspoon salt

½ teaspoon Italian seasoning

3 medium unpeeled russet potatoes (about 1 pound), halved lengthwise and thinly sliced

2 cups packed torn stemmed kale leaves

1 cup half-and-half or whipping cream

*Or use sausage links and remove from casings.

1 Heat oil in large saucepan or Dutch oven over medium-high heat. Add sausage; cook until sausage begins to brown, stirring to break up meat. Add onion and garlic; cook about 5 minutes or until onion is softened and sausage is browned, stirring occasionally.

2 Stir in flour until blended. Add broth, salt and Italian seasoning; bring to a boil. Stir in potatoes and kale. Reduce heat to medium-low; cook 15 to 20 minutes or until potatoes are fork-tender. Reduce heat to low; stir in half-and-half. Cook about 5 minutes or until heated through.

SAUSAGE AND LENTIL SOUP

MAKES 4 TO 6 SERVINGS

8 ounces spicy Italian sausage

1 onion, chopped

2 cloves garlic, minced

1 stalk celery, chopped

1 carrot, chopped

1 small zucchini, chopped

3 to 3½ cups chicken broth, divided

1 can (about 14 ounces) diced tomatoes

1 cup dried lentils, rinsed and sorted

½ teaspoon salt

½ teaspoon dried oregano

½ teaspoon dried basil

¼ teaspoon dried thyme

¼ teaspoon black pepper

Chopped fresh basil and grated Parmesan cheese (optional)

1 Brown sausage in large saucepan or Dutch oven over medium-high heat, stirring to break up meat. Add onion; cook and stir 3 minutes or until onion begins to soften. Add garlic; cook and stir 1 minute. Add celery, carrot and zucchini; cook 3 minutes, stirring occasionally.

2 Stir in 3 cups broth, tomatoes, lentils, salt, oregano, dried basil, thyme and pepper; bring to a boil. Reduce heat to low; cover and cook about 1 hour or until lentils are tender. Add additional broth if needed to thin soup. Garnish with fresh basil and cheese.

CHICKEN AND GNOCCHI SOUP

MAKES 6 TO 8 SERVINGS

¼ cup (½ stick) butter

1 tablespoon extra virgin olive oil

1 cup finely diced onion

2 stalks celery, finely chopped

2 cloves garlic, minced

¼ cup all-purpose flour

4 cups half-and-half

1 can (about 14 ounces) chicken broth

1 teaspoon salt

½ teaspoon dried thyme

½ teaspoon dried parsley flakes

¼ teaspoon ground nutmeg

1 package (about 16 ounces) gnocchi

1 package (6 ounces) fully cooked chicken strips, chopped *or* 1 cup diced cooked chicken

1 cup shredded carrots

1 cup coarsely chopped fresh spinach leaves

1 Melt butter in large saucepan or Dutch oven over medium heat; add oil. Add onion, celery and garlic; cook about 10 minutes or until vegetables are softened and onion is translucent, stirring occasionally.

2 Whisk in flour; cook and stir about 1 minute. Whisk in half-and-half; cook about 15 minutes or until thickened.

3 Whisk in broth, salt, thyme, parsley flakes and nutmeg; simmer 10 minutes or until slightly thickened. Add gnocchi, chicken, carrots and spinach; cook about 5 minutes or until gnocchi is heated through.

BAKED POTATO SOUP

MAKES 6 TO 8 SERVINGS

3 medium russet potatoes (about 1 pound)

¼ cup (½ stick) butter

1 cup chopped onion

½ cup all-purpose flour

4 cups chicken or vegetable broth

1½ cups instant mashed potato flakes

1 cup water

1 cup half-and-half

1 teaspoon salt

½ teaspoon dried basil

½ teaspoon dried thyme

¼ teaspoon black pepper

1 cup (4 ounces) shredded Cheddar cheese

4 slices bacon, crisp-cooked and crumbled

1 green onion, chopped

1 Preheat oven to 400°F. Scrub potatoes and prick in several places with fork. Place in baking pan; bake 1 hour. Cool completely; peel and cut into ½-inch pieces. (Potatoes can be prepared several days in advance; refrigerate until ready to use.)

2 Melt butter in large saucepan or Dutch oven over medium heat. Add onion; cook and stir 3 minutes or until softened. Whisk in flour until well blended; cook and stir 1 minute. Gradually whisk in broth until well blended. Stir in mashed potato flakes, water, half-and-half, salt, basil, thyme and pepper; bring to a boil over medium-high heat. Reduce heat to medium; cook 5 minutes.

3 Stir in baked potato cubes; cook 10 to 15 minutes or until soup is thickened and heated through. Ladle into bowls; top with cheese, bacon and green onion.

CHICKEN ENCHILADA SOUP

MAKES 8 TO 10 SERVINGS

2 tablespoons vegetable oil, divided

1½ pounds boneless skinless chicken breasts, cut into ½-inch pieces

½ cup chopped onion

2 cloves garlic, minced

2 cans (about 14 ounces each) chicken broth

3 cups water, divided

1 cup masa harina

1 package (16 ounces) pasteurized process cheese, cubed

1 can (10 ounces) mild red enchilada sauce

1 teaspoon chili powder

½ teaspoon salt

½ teaspoon ground cumin

Chopped fresh tomatoes

Crispy tortilla strips*

*If tortilla strips are unavailable, crumble tortilla chips into bite-size pieces.

1 Heat 1 tablespoon oil in large saucepan or Dutch oven over medium-high heat. Add chicken; cook and stir 10 minutes or until no longer pink. Transfer chicken to large bowl with slotted spoon; drain fat from saucepan.

2 Heat remaining 1 tablespoon oil in same saucepan over medium-high heat. Add onion and garlic; cook and stir 3 minutes or until softened. Stir in broth.

3 Whisk 2 cups water into masa in large bowl until smooth. Whisk mixture into broth in saucepan. Stir in process cheese, remaining 1 cup water, enchilada sauce, chili powder, salt and cumin; bring to a boil over high heat. Add chicken. Reduce heat to medium-low; cook 30 minutes, stirring frequently. Ladle into bowls; top with tomatoes and tortilla strips.

CREAMY ONION SOUP

MAKES 4 SERVINGS

6 tablespoons (¾ stick) butter, divided

1 large sweet onion, thinly sliced (about 3 cups)

1 can (about 14 ounces) chicken broth

2 cubes chicken bouillon

¼ teaspoon black pepper

¼ cup all-purpose flour

1½ cups milk

1½ cups (6 ounces) shredded Colby-Jack cheese

Chopped fresh parsley (optional)

1 Melt 2 tablespoons butter in large saucepan or Dutch oven over medium heat. Add onion; cook 10 minutes or until soft and translucent, stirring occasionally. Add broth, bouillon and pepper; cook until bouillon is dissolved and mixture is heated through.

2 Meanwhile, melt remaining 4 tablespoons butter in medium saucepan. Whisk in flour; cook and stir 1 minute. Gradually whisk in milk until well blended. Cook about 10 minutes or until very thick, stirring occasionally.

3 Add milk mixture to soup; cook over medium-low heat 5 to 10 minutes or until thickened, stirring occasionally. Stir in cheese; cook 5 minutes or until melted and smooth. Ladle into bowls; garnish with parsley.

MINESTRONE SOUP

MAKES 4 TO 6 SERVINGS

1 tablespoon olive oil

½ cup chopped onion

1 stalk celery, diced

1 carrot, diced

2 cloves garlic, minced

2 cups vegetable broth

1½ cups water

1 bay leaf

¾ teaspoon salt

½ teaspoon dried basil

½ teaspoon dried oregano

¼ teaspoon dried thyme

¼ teaspoon sugar

Ground black pepper

1 can (about 15 ounces) dark red kidney beans, rinsed and drained

1 can (about 15 ounces) navy beans or cannellini beans, rinsed and drained

1 can (about 14 ounces) diced tomatoes

1 cup diced zucchini (about 1 small)

½ cup uncooked small shell pasta

½ cup frozen cut green beans

¼ cup dry red wine

1 cup packed chopped fresh spinach

Grated Parmesan cheese (optional)

1 Heat oil in large saucepan or Dutch oven over medium-high heat. Add onion, celery, carrot and garlic; cook and stir 5 to 7 minutes or until vegetables are tender. Add broth, water, bay leaf, salt, basil, oregano, thyme, sugar and pepper; bring to a boil.

2 Stir in kidney beans, navy beans, tomatoes, zucchini, pasta, green beans and wine; cook 10 minutes, stirring occasionally.

3 Add spinach; cook 2 minutes or until pasta and zucchini are tender. Ladle into bowls; garnish with cheese.

SALADS

WEDGE SALAD
MAKES 4 SERVINGS

DRESSING

- ¾ cup mayonnaise
- ½ cup buttermilk
- 1 cup crumbled blue cheese, divided
- 1 clove garlic, minced
- ½ teaspoon sugar
- ⅛ teaspoon onion powder
- ⅛ teaspoon salt
- ⅛ teaspoon black pepper

SALAD

- 1 head iceberg lettuce
- 1 large tomato, diced (about 1 cup)
- ½ small red onion, cut into thin rings
- ½ cup crumbled crisp-cooked bacon (6 to 8 slices)

1 For dressing, combine mayonnaise, buttermilk, ½ cup cheese, garlic, sugar, onion powder, salt and pepper in food processor or blender; process until smooth.

2 Cut lettuce into quarters through the stem end; remove stem from each wedge. Place wedges on individual serving plates; top with dressing. Sprinkle with tomato, onion, remaining ½ cup cheese and bacon.

PECAN-CRUSTED CHICKEN SALAD

MAKES 4 SERVINGS

CHICKEN

- ½ cup all-purpose flour
- ½ cup milk
- 1 egg
- ⅔ cup corn flake crumbs
- ⅔ cup finely chopped pecans
- ¾ teaspoon salt
- 4 boneless skinless chicken breasts (1¼ to 1½ pounds total)

DRESSING

- ⅓ cup balsamic vinegar
- 1 tablespoon Dijon mustard
- 1 tablespoon sugar
- 1 teaspoon minced garlic
- ½ teaspoon salt
- ⅔ cup canola oil

SALAD

- 10 cups mixed greens (1-pound package)
- 2 cans (11 ounces each) mandarin oranges, drained
- 1 cup sliced celery
- ¾ cup dried cranberries
- ½ cup glazed pecans*
- ½ cup crumbled blue cheese

Glazed or candied pecans or walnuts can be found in the produce section of the supermarket along with other salad convenience items.

1 Preheat oven to 400°F. Line baking sheet with foil; spray with nonstick cooking spray.

2 Place flour in shallow dish. Beat milk and egg in another shallow dish. Combine corn flake crumbs, chopped pecans and salt in third shallow dish. Dip both sides of chicken in flour, then in egg mixture, letting excess drip back into dish. Roll in crumb mixture to coat completely, pressing crumbs into chicken to adhere. Place on prepared baking sheet.

3 Bake 20 minutes or until chicken is no longer pink in center. Cool completely before slicing. (Chicken can be prepared several hours in advance and refrigerated.)

4 Meanwhile, prepare dressing. Combine vinegar, mustard, sugar, garlic and salt in medium bowl; mix well. Slowly add oil, whisking until well blended.

5 For salad, combine mixed greens, mandarin oranges, celery, cranberries, glazed pecans and cheese in large bowl. Add two thirds of dressing; toss gently to coat. Divide salad among 4 plates. Cut chicken breasts diagonally into ½-inch slices; arrange over salads. Serve with remaining dressing.

CHICKEN WALDORF SALAD

MAKES 4 SERVINGS

DRESSING

⅓ cup balsamic vinegar

2 tablespoons Dijon mustard

2 teaspoons minced garlic

½ teaspoon salt

¼ teaspoon black pepper

⅔ cup extra virgin olive oil

SALAD

8 cups mixed greens

1 large Granny Smith apple, cut into ½-inch pieces

⅔ cup diced celery

⅔ cup halved red seedless grapes

12 to 16 ounces sliced grilled chicken breasts

½ cup candied walnuts

½ cup crumbled blue cheese

1 For dressing, combine vinegar, mustard, garlic, salt and pepper in medium bowl; mix well. Slowly add oil, whisking until well blended.

2 For salad, combine mixed greens, apple, celery and grapes in large bowl. Add half of dressing; toss to coat. Top with chicken, walnuts and cheese; drizzle with additional dressing.

HOUSE SALAD

MAKES 4 SERVINGS

DRESSING

- ½ cup mayonnaise
- ½ cup white wine vinegar
- ¼ cup grated Parmesan cheese
- 1 tablespoon olive oil
- 1 tablespoon lemon juice
- 1 tablespoon corn syrup
- 1 clove garlic, minced
- ¾ teaspoon Italian seasoning
- ½ teaspoon salt
- ½ teaspoon black pepper

SALAD

- 1 package (10 ounces) Italian salad blend
- 2 plum tomatoes, thinly sliced
- 1 cup croutons
- ½ cup thinly sliced red or green bell pepper
- ½ cup thinly sliced red onion
- ¼ cup sliced black olives
- Pepperoncini (optional)

1 For dressing, whisk mayonnaise, vinegar, cheese, oil, lemon juice, corn syrup, garlic, Italian seasoning, salt and pepper in medium bowl until well blended.

2 For salad, place salad blend in large bowl; top with tomatoes, croutons, bell pepper, onion, olives and pepperoncini, if desired. Add dressing; toss to coat.

STRAWBERRY POPPY SEED CHICKEN SALAD

MAKES 4 SERVINGS

DRESSING

- ¼ cup white wine vinegar
- 2 tablespoons orange juice
- 1 tablespoon sugar
- 2 teaspoons poppy seeds
- 1½ teaspoons Dijon mustard
- ½ teaspoon salt
- ½ teaspoon minced dried onion
- ½ cup vegetable oil

SALAD

- 8 cups romaine lettuce
- 1 package (12 to 16 ounces) grilled or roasted chicken breast strips
- ¾ cup fresh pineapple chunks
- ¾ cup sliced fresh strawberries
- ¾ cup fresh blueberries
- 1 navel orange, peeled and sectioned *or* 1 can (11 ounces) mandarin oranges, drained
- ¼ cup chopped toasted pecans

1 For dressing, combine vinegar, orange juice, sugar, poppy seeds, mustard, salt and dried onion in small bowl; mix well. Slowly add oil, whisking until well blended.

2 For salad, combine romaine and two thirds of dressing in large bowl; toss gently to coat. Divide salad among 4 plates, top with chicken, pineapple, strawberries, blueberries, oranges and pecans. Serve with remaining dressing.

STEAKHOUSE CHOPPED SALAD
MAKES 8 TO 10 SERVINGS

DRESSING

Italian Seasoning Mix (recipe follows) *or* 1 package (about 2 tablespoons) Italian salad dressing mix

⅓ cup white balsamic vinegar

¼ cup Dijon mustard

⅔ cup extra virgin olive oil

SALAD

1 medium head iceberg lettuce, chopped

1 medium head romaine lettuce, chopped

1 can (about 14 ounces) hearts of palm or artichoke hearts, quartered lengthwise then sliced crosswise

1 large avocado, diced

1½ cups crumbled blue cheese

2 hard-cooked eggs, chopped

1 ripe tomato, chopped

½ small red onion, finely chopped

12 slices bacon, crisp-cooked and crumbled

1 For dressing, prepare Italian Seasoning Mix. Whisk vinegar, mustard and dressing mix in small bowl. Slowly add oil, whisking until well blended. Set aside until ready to use. (Dressing can be made up to 1 week in advance and refrigerated.)

2 For salad, combine lettuce, hearts of palm, avocado, cheese, eggs, tomato, onion and bacon in large bowl. Add dressing; toss to coat.

ITALIAN SEASONING MIX
MAKES ABOUT 2½ TABLESPOONS

1½ teaspoons salt

1½ teaspoons dried oregano

¾ teaspoon sugar

¾ teaspoon onion powder

¾ teaspoon dried parsley flakes

½ teaspoon garlic powder

¼ teaspoon dried basil

¼ teaspoon black pepper

⅛ teaspoon dried thyme

⅛ teaspoon celery salt

Combine all ingredients in small bowl; mix well.

SHRIMP AND SPINACH SALAD

MAKES 4 SERVINGS

DRESSING

- 3 to 4 slices bacon
- ¼ cup red wine vinegar
- ½ teaspoon cornstarch
- ¼ cup olive oil
- ¼ cup sugar
- ¼ teaspoon salt
- ¼ teaspoon black pepper
- ¼ teaspoon liquid smoke

SHRIMP

- 2 teaspoons black pepper
- 1 teaspoon salt
- 1 teaspoon garlic powder
- ½ teaspoon sugar
- ½ teaspoon onion powder
- ½ teaspoon ground sage
- ½ teaspoon paprika
- 20 to 24 large raw shrimp, peeled and deveined
- 2 tablespoons olive oil

SALAD

- 8 cups packed torn stemmed spinach
- 1 tomato, diced
- ½ red onion, thinly sliced
- ½ cup sliced roasted red peppers

1 For dressing, cook bacon in large skillet over medium heat until crisp. Drain on paper towel-lined plate. Drain all but 3 tablespoons drippings from skillet. Crumble bacon; set aside.

2 Heat skillet with drippings over medium heat. Whisk vinegar into cornstarch in small bowl until smooth. Whisk cornstarch mixture into drippings in skillet; cook 1 to 2 minutes or until slightly thickened, whisking constantly. Remove from heat; pour into small bowl or glass measuring cup. Whisk in ¼ cup oil, ¼ cup sugar, ¼ teaspoon salt, ¼ teaspoon black pepper and liquid smoke until well blended. Wipe out skillet with paper towel.

3 For shrimp, combine 2 teaspoons black pepper, 1 teaspoon salt, garlic powder, ½ teaspoon sugar, onion powder, sage and paprika in medium bowl; mix well. Add shrimp; toss to coat.

4 Heat 2 tablespoons oil in same skillet over medium-high heat. Add shrimp; cook 2 to 3 minutes per side or until shrimp are pink and opaque.

5 For salad, combine spinach, tomato, onion and roasted peppers in large bowl. Add two thirds of dressing; toss to coat. Top with shrimp and crumbled bacon; serve with remaining dressing.

BBQ CHICKEN SALAD

MAKES 4 SERVINGS

DRESSING

- ¾ cup light or regular mayonnaise
- ⅓ cup buttermilk
- ¼ cup sour cream
- 1 tablespoon white wine vinegar
- 1 teaspoon sugar
- ¼ teaspoon salt
- ¼ teaspoon garlic powder
- ¼ teaspoon onion powder
- ¼ teaspoon dried parsley flakes
- ¼ teaspoon dried dill weed
- ¼ teaspoon black pepper

SALAD

- 12 to 16 ounces grilled chicken breast strips
- ½ cup barbecue sauce
- 4 cups chopped romaine lettuce
- 4 cups chopped iceberg lettuce
- 2 medium tomatoes, seeded and chopped
- ¾ cup canned or thawed frozen corn, drained
- ¾ cup diced jicama
- ¾ cup (3 ounces) shredded Monterey Jack cheese
- ¼ cup chopped fresh cilantro
- 2 green onions, sliced
- 1 cup crispy tortilla strips*

*If tortilla strips are unavailable, crumble tortilla chips into bite-size pieces.

1 For dressing, whisk mayonnaise, buttermilk, sour cream, vinegar, sugar, salt, garlic powder, onion powder, parsley flakes, dill and pepper in medium bowl until well blended. Cover and refrigerate until ready to serve.

2 For salad, cut chicken strips into ½-inch pieces. Combine chicken and barbecue sauce in medium bowl; toss to coat.

3 Combine lettuce, tomatoes, corn, jicama, cheese and cilantro in large bowl. Add two thirds of dressing; toss to coat. Add remaining dressing if necessary. Divide salad among 4 plates; top with chicken, green onions and tortilla strips.

SANDWICHES

SOUTHWEST TURKEY SANDWICH
MAKES 4 SERVINGS

½ cup mayonnaise

1 tablespoon minced chipotle pepper in adobo sauce

1½ teaspoons lime juice

1 round loaf (16 ounces) cheese focaccia or cheese bread

1½ cups mixed greens

12 ounces sliced smoked turkey

½ red onion, thinly sliced

1 Combine mayonnaise, chipotle pepper and lime juice in small bowl; mix well.

2 Cut bread in half horizontally; spread cut sides of bread with mayonnaise mixture. Top bottom half of loaf with mixed greens, turkey, onion and top half of loaf. Cut into wedges.

GUACAMOLE BURGERS

MAKES 4 SERVINGS

1 small avocado

2 tablespoons finely chopped tomato

1 tablespoon chopped fresh cilantro

2 teaspoons lime juice, divided

1 teaspoon minced jalapeño pepper

¼ teaspoon salt, divided

2 tablespoons sour cream

2 tablespoons mayonnaise

½ teaspoon ground cumin

4 teaspoons vegetable oil, divided

1 medium onion, cut into thin slices

1 small green bell pepper, cut into thin slices

1 small red bell pepper, cut into thin slices

1¼ pounds ground beef

Salt and black pepper

4 slices Monterey Jack cheese

4 hamburger buns, split and toasted

1 can (4 ounces) diced fire-roasted jalapeño peppers, drained

1 Mash avocado in medium bowl. Stir in tomato, cilantro, 1 teaspoon lime juice, minced jalepeño and ⅛ teaspoon salt; mix well. Cover and refrigerate until ready to use. Combine sour cream, mayonnaise, remaining 1 teaspoon lime juice and cumin in small bowl; mix well. Cover and refrigerate until ready to use.

2 Heat 2 teaspoons oil in large skillet over medium-high heat. Add onion; cook about 10 minutes or until onion is very tender and begins to turn golden, stirring occasionally. (Add a few teaspoons water to skillet if onion begins to burn.) Remove to bowl. Add remaining 2 teaspoons oil to skillet. Add bell peppers; cook and stir 5 minutes or until tender. Remove to bowl with onion; season vegetables with remaining ⅛ teaspoon salt.

3 Preheat grill or broiler. Shape beef into 4 (5-inch) patties; sprinkle both sides generously with salt and black pepper. Grill or broil patties about 5 minutes per side or until cooked through (160°F). Top patties with cheese slices during last minute of cooking.

4 Spread sour cream mixture over bottom halves of buns. Top with onion and bell peppers, burgers, guacamole, fire-roasted jalapeños and top halves of buns.

SANDWICHES

MEDITERRANEAN VEGETABLE SANDWICH

MAKES 4 SANDWICHES

½ cup plain hummus

½ jalapeño pepper, seeded and minced

¼ cup minced fresh cilantro

8 slices whole wheat bread

4 leaves lettuce (leaf or Bibb lettuce)

2 tomatoes, thinly sliced

½ cucumber, thinly sliced

½ red onion, thinly sliced

½ cup thinly sliced peppadew peppers or sweet Italian peppers

4 tablespoons crumbled feta cheese

1 Combine hummus, jalapeño and cilantro in small bowl; mix well.

2 Spread about 1 tablespoon hummus mixture on one side of each bread slice. Layer half of bread slices with lettuce, tomatoes, cucumber, onion, peppadew peppers and cheese; top with remaining bread slices. Cut sandwiches in half.

CUBAN PORK SANDWICH

MAKES 4 SANDWICHES

⅓ cup orange juice

3 tablespoons lime juice

1 small onion, finely chopped
  (½ cup)

3 tablespoons olive oil

6 cloves garlic, minced

2 teaspoons ground cumin

2 teaspoons dried oregano

1 teaspoon salt

1 teaspoon black pepper

2 pounds boneless pork shoulder

4 Cuban sandwich rolls, split*

⅓ cup mayonnaise

⅓ cup yellow mustard

8 ounces sliced Swiss cheese

8 ounces sliced honey ham

8 long thin dill pickle slices

If Cuban rolls are unavailable, substitute a long French or Italian loaf (at least 16 ounces), split in half horizontally and cut into 4 pieces.

1 Combine orange juice, lime juice, onion, oil, garlic, cumin, oregano, salt and pepper in medium bowl; mix well. Place pork in large resealable food storage bag. Pour marinade over pork; seal bag and turn to coat. Marinate in refrigerator at least 2 hours or overnight.

2 Preheat oven to 325°F. Line shallow roasting pan or baking dish with heavy-duty foil. Place pork in prepared pan with half of marinade; discard remaining marinade. Roast about 3 hours or until pork is tender and temperature reaches 160°F. Let stand at least 15 minutes before slicing. (Pork can be prepared in advance and refrigerated.)

3 Slice pork. (About half of pork is needed for sandwiches; reserve remaining pork for another use.) Spread both cut sides of rolls with mayonnaise, then mustard. Top bottom halves of rolls with half of cheese, ham, pickles, pork, remaining cheese and top halves of rolls.

4 Cook sandwiches in sandwich press, grill pan or hot skillet over medium heat until bread is lightly browned and crisp. (If using grill pan or skillet, use second skillet to press down to compress sandwiches; cook about 5 minutes per side until bread is crisp.)

CLASSIC PATTY MELTS

MAKES 4 SERVINGS

5 tablespoons butter, divided

2 large yellow onions, thinly sliced

¾ teaspoon plus pinch of salt, divided

1 pound ground chuck (80% lean)

½ teaspoon garlic powder

½ teaspoon onion powder

¼ teaspoon black pepper

8 slices marble rye bread

½ cup Thousand Island dressing

8 slices deli American or Swiss cheese

1 Melt 2 tablespoons butter in large skillet over medium heat. Add onions and pinch of salt; cook about 20 minutes or until onions are very soft and golden brown, stirring occasionally. Remove to small bowl; wipe out skillet with paper towel.

2 Combine beef, remaining ¾ teaspoon salt, garlic powder, onion powder and pepper in medium bowl; mix gently. Shape into 4 patties about the size and shape of bread slices and ¼ to ½ inch thick.

3 Melt 1 tablespoon butter in same skillet over medium-high heat. Add patties, two at a time; cook about about 3 minutes or until bottoms are browned, pressing down gently to form crust. Turn patties and cook 3 minutes or until browned. Remove patties to plate; wipe out skillet with paper towel.

4 Spread one side of each bread slice with dressing. Top 4 bread slices with cheese slice, patty, caramelized onions, another cheese slice and remaining bread slices.

5 Melt 1 tablespoon butter in same skillet over medium heat. Add two sandwiches to skillet; cook about 4 minutes or until golden brown, pressing down to crisp bread. Turn sandwiches and cook 4 minutes or until golden brown and cheese is melted. Repeat with remaining sandwiches and 1 tablespoon butter.

THE GREAT REUBEN SANDWICH

MAKES 2 SANDWICHES

¼ cup Thousand Island dressing (see Tip)

4 slices rye bread

8 ounces thinly sliced corned beef or pastrami

4 slices Swiss cheese

½ cup sauerkraut, well drained

2 tablespoons butter

1 Spread dressing on one side of each bread slice. Top 2 bread slices with corned beef, cheese, sauerkraut and remaining bread slices.

2 Melt butter in large skillet over medium heat. Cook sandwiches about 6 minutes per side or until cheese is melted and bread is lightly browned, pressing down with spatula to crisp bread slightly. Serve immediately.

TIP

If you don't have Thousand Island dressing, you can make your own by combining 2 tablespoons mayonnaise, 2 tablespoons sweet pickle relish and 1 tablespoon cocktail sauce.

THE ROYAL BURGER

MAKES 2 SERVINGS

1 teaspoon Royal Seasoning
(recipe follows), divided

4 slices bacon

12 ounces ground beef

2 slices deli American cheese

2 eggs

Salt and black pepper

2 sesame seed buns, split
and toasted

2 tablespoons mayonnaise

½ cup shredded lettuce

4 slices ripe tomato

1 Prepare Royal Seasoning.

2 Cook bacon in large skillet over medium heat; drain on paper towel-lined plate. Pour off all but 1 teaspoon drippings from skillet. (Reserve some of bacon drippings for frying eggs, if desired.)

3 Combine beef and ¾ teaspoon Royal Seasoning in medium bowl; mix gently. Shape into 2 (5-inch) patties. Sprinkle both sides of patties with remaining ¼ teaspoon seasoning mix.

4 Return skillet to medium heat. Cook patties about 5 minutes per side or until cooked through (160°F).* Top each burger with cheese slice during last minute of cooking.

5 While burgers are cooking, heat 2 teaspoons reserved bacon drippings or butter in another large skillet or griddle over medium heat. Crack eggs into skillet; cook 3 to 4 minutes or until whites are set and yolks begin to thicken and firm around edges. Season with salt and pepper.

6 Spread cut sides of buns with mayonnaise. Top bottom buns with lettuce, burgers, bacon, tomato, eggs and top buns.

*Patties can also be grilled or broiled 5 minutes per side or until cooked through.

ROYAL SEASONING

MAKES ABOUT ⅓ CUP

2 tablespoons salt

1½ tablespoons paprika

1 tablespoon garlic powder

½ tablespoon onion powder

½ tablespoon chili powder

¾ teaspoon ground cumin

¾ teaspoon dried basil

¾ teaspoon black pepper

¼ teaspoon dried oregano

Combine all ingredients in small bowl; mix well. Store in airtight container. Seasoning mix can be used for steaks, chicken and vegetables in addition to burgers.

MONTE CRISTO SANDWICHES

MAKES 4 SERVINGS

12 thin slices honey wheat or whole wheat bread

4 ounces sliced deli turkey breast

4 thin slices (2 ounces) Swiss cheese

4 ounces smoked sliced deli ham

4 thin slices (2 ounces) deli American cheese

2 eggs

¼ cup milk

⅛ teaspoon salt

Pinch of ground nutmeg

2 to 3 tablespoons butter

Powdered sugar

Raspberry preserves

1 Preheat oven to 450°F. Line baking sheet with foil.

2 For each sandwich, layer ¼ of turkey and 1 Swiss cheese slice on 1 bread slice; top with second bread slice, ¼ of ham, 1 American cheese slice and third bread slice. Press sandwiches together gently.

3 Beat eggs, milk, salt and nutmeg in shallow dish until blended. Dip both sides of each sandwich briefly in egg mixture, letting excess drip back into dish.

4 Melt 1 tablespoon butter in large nonstick skillet over medium heat. Cook two sandwiches at a time 2 to 3 minutes per side or until browned, adding additional butter to skillet as needed. Transfer sandwiches to prepared baking sheet.

5 Bake 5 to 7 minutes or until sandwiches are heated through and cheese is melted. Cut sandwiches in half diagonally; sprinkle lightly with powdered sugar. Serve immediately with raspberry preserves.

NOTE

The restaurant version uses a thicker batter and deep fries the sandwiches, but this triple decker recipe is much quicker and easier to make at home.

TUSCAN PORTOBELLO MELT

MAKES 2 SERVINGS

1 portobello mushroom cap, thinly sliced

½ small red onion, thinly sliced

½ cup grape tomatoes

1 tablespoon olive oil

1 teaspoon balsamic vinegar

⅛ teaspoon salt

⅛ teaspoon dried thyme

⅛ teaspoon black pepper

4 slices sourdough bread

2 tablespoons butter, softened

2 teaspoons Dijon mustard

2 slices provolone cheese

2 slices Monterey Jack cheese

1 Preheat broiler. Combine mushroom, onion and tomatoes in small baking pan. Drizzle with oil and vinegar; sprinkle with salt, thyme and pepper. Toss to coat. Spread vegetables in single layer in pan.

2 Broil about 6 minutes or until vegetables are softened and browned, stirring once.

3 Heat medium skillet over medium heat. Spread some of butter over one side of each bread slice. Place buttered side down in skillet; cook 2 minutes or until bread is toasted. Transfer bread to cutting board, toasted sides up.

4 Spread mustard over 2 bread slices; top with provolone cheese, vegetables, Monterey Jack cheese and remaining bread slices, toasted sides down. Spread remaining butter on outside of sandwiches. Cook in same skillet over medium heat about 5 minutes or until bread is toasted and cheese is melted, turning once.

SOUTHWESTERN BLT

MAKES 2 SERVINGS

6 slices thick-cut applewood
   smoked bacon

¼ cup mayonnaise

1 teaspoon lime juice

¼ teaspoon ground chipotle pepper

¼ teaspoon ground cumin

1 large ripe tomato

2 pretzel rolls, split and toasted

½ cup shredded lettuce

1 Cook bacon in large skillet over medium heat; drain on paper towel-lined plate.

2 Combine mayonnaise, lime juice, chipotle pepper and cumin in small bowl; mix well.

3 Cut tomato into 4 thick slices. Spread cut sides of rolls with mayonnaise mixture. Top bottom halves of rolls with lettuce, tomato, bacon and top halves of rolls.

MAIN DISHES

FETTUCCINE ALFREDO
MAKES 4 SERVINGS

12 ounces uncooked fettuccine

⅔ cup whipping cream

6 tablespoons (¾ stick) butter

½ teaspoon salt

Generous dash white pepper

Generous dash ground nutmeg

1 cup grated Parmesan cheese

2 tablespoons chopped fresh Italian parsley

1 Cook pasta according to package directions. Drain well; cover and keep warm in saucepan.

2 Meanwhile, heat cream and butter in large heavy skillet over medium-low heat until butter melts and mixture bubbles, stirring frequently. Cook and stir 2 minutes. Stir in salt, pepper and nutmeg. Remove from heat; gradually stir in cheese until well blended and smooth. Return to low heat, if necessary; do not let sauce bubble or cheese will become lumpy and tough.

3 Pour sauce over pasta. Cook and stir over low heat 2 to 3 minutes or until sauce is thickened and pasta is evenly coated. Sprinkle with parsley. Serve immediately.

SPICY ORANGE CHICKEN

MAKES 4 SERVINGS

2 oranges

¼ cup mild-flavored molasses

1 tablespoon soy sauce

2 teaspoons cornstarch

¾ cup all-purpose flour

½ teaspoon salt

¼ teaspoon baking powder

¾ cup water

1 pound boneless skinless chicken breasts or thighs, cut into 1-inch pieces

Vegetable oil for frying

1 teaspoon chili oil

4 whole dried chile peppers

2 cloves garlic, minced

1½ teaspoons finely chopped fresh ginger

Hot cooked rice

1 Remove ½-inch wide strips of peel from 1 orange with vegetable peeler. Slice peel into 1-inch-long pieces; set aside. (Remove colored portion of skin only; white pith has a bitter taste.)

2 Juice oranges to measure ½ cup juice. Combine orange juice, molasses, soy sauce and cornstarch in small bowl; set aside.

3 Combine flour, salt and baking powder in medium bowl. Whisk in water to form smooth batter. Add chicken; stir to coat.

4 Heat about 3 cups vegetable oil in wok or deep heavy saucepan over medium-high heat to 375°F; adjust heat to maintain temperature. Shake off excess batter from one third of chicken; carefully add chicken to wok.

5 Cook about 4 minutes or until chicken is golden brown and cooked through, stirring occasionally to break up pieces with spoon. Remove chicken with slotted spoon to paper towel-lined plate. Repeat with remaining chicken, reheating oil between batches.

6 Pour off all oil from wok. Reheat wok over medium-high heat until hot; add chili oil. Add orange peel, chile peppers, garlic and ginger; cook and stir 30 seconds to 1 minute or until fragrant.

7 Stir cornstarch mixture; add to wok. Cook and stir until sauce boils and thickens. Return chicken to wok; mix well. Serve with rice.

BEER-BATTERED FISH AND CHIPS

MAKES 4 SERVINGS

¾ cup all-purpose flour, plus additional for dusting fish

½ cup flat beer

Vegetable oil

3 large or 4 medium russet potatoes

1 egg, separated

1 pound cod fillets

Salt

Prepared tartar sauce

Lemon wedges

1 Combine ¾ cup flour, beer and 2 teaspoons oil in small bowl; mix well. Cover and refrigerate 30 minutes to 2 hours.

2 Peel potatoes and cut into ¾-inch sticks. Place in large bowl of cold water. Heat at least 2 inches of oil in deep heavy saucepan or deep fryer over medium heat to 320°F; adjust heat to maintain temperature. Drain and thoroughly dry potatoes. Fry in batches 3 minutes or until slightly softened but not browned. Drain on paper towel-lined plate.

3 Stir egg yolk into cold flour mixture. Beat egg white in medium bowl with electric mixer at medium-high speed until soft peaks form. Fold egg white into flour mixture. Season batter with pinch of salt.

4 Preheat oven to 200°F. Heat oil to 365°F. Cut fish into pieces about 6 inches long and 2 to 3 inches wide. Remove any pin bones. Dust fish with flour; dip fish into batter, shaking off excess. Lower carefully into oil; cook 4 to 6 minutes or until batter is browned and fish is cooked through, turning once. Cook fish in batches; do not crowd saucepan. (Allow temperature of oil to return to 365°F between batches.) Drain on paper towel-lined plate; keep warm in oven.

5 Return potatoes to hot oil; cook in batches 5 minutes or until browned and crisp. Drain on paper towel-lined plate; sprinkle with salt. Serve fish with potatoes, tartar sauce and lemon wedges.

THAI CHICKEN PIZZA
MAKES 4 SERVINGS

CRUST

- 1 package (¼ ounce) rapid-rise active dry yeast
- 1 teaspoon granulated sugar
- 1 cup warm water (120°F)
- 3 cups bread flour
- 2 tablespoons olive oil
- 1 teaspoon salt

SAUCE

- ½ cup creamy peanut butter
- ½ cup hoisin sauce
- 2 tablespoons packed brown sugar
- 2 tablespoons dark sesame oil
- 1 tablespoon minced fresh ginger
- 1 tablespoon water
- 1 tablespoon unseasoned rice vinegar
- 1 tablespoon soy sauce
- 2 cloves garlic, minced
- 1 teaspoon onion powder
- 1 teaspoon sriracha sauce

TOPPING

- 1 tablespoon vegetable oil
- 1 pound boneless skinless chicken breasts, cut into ½-inch pieces
- 2 cups (8 ounces) shredded mozzarella cheese
- 4 green onions, thinly sliced diagonally
- 1 large carrot, julienned
- ½ cup bean sprouts
- 2 tablespoons chopped roasted peanuts
- 2 tablespoons minced fresh cilantro

1 For crust, dissolve yeast and granulated sugar in warm water in large bowl of stand mixer. Let stand 5 minutes or until bubbly. Stir in flour, olive oil and salt until rough dough forms. Knead at low speed with dough hook 5 minutes or until dough is smooth and elastic. Shape dough into a ball. Place in large greased bowl; turn to grease top. Cover and let rise in warm place about 1 hour or until doubled in size.

2 For sauce, combine peanut butter, hoisin sauce, brown sugar, sesame oil, ginger, 1 tablespoon water, vinegar, soy sauce, garlic, onion powder and sriracha in small saucepan; cook over medium-low heat 3 to 5 minutes or until sauce is smooth and dark, whisking frequently. Remove from heat.

3 For topping, heat vegetable oil in large skillet over medium-high heat. Add chicken; cook about 5 minutes or until cooked through, stirring occasionally. Add ½ cup sauce; cook and stir over medium heat 1 minute or until chicken is glazed. Remove from heat.

4 Preheat oven to 500°F. Line two large baking sheets with parchment paper. Punch down dough; cut in half and shape into two balls. Cover and let rest 10 minutes. Roll out dough on lightly floured surface into 2 (12-inch) circles. Spread ¼ cup sauce over each circle to within ½ inch of edge; sprinkle each pizza with ½ cup cheese. Top evenly with chicken, green onions, carrot and bean sprouts. Top with remaining cheese.

5 Bake about 10 minutes or until crust is golden brown and cheese is melted. Sprinkle with peanuts and cilantro. Cut into wedges.

FRENCH QUARTER STEAKS

MAKES 2 SERVINGS

½ cup water

2 tablespoons Worcestershire sauce

2 tablespoons soy sauce

1 tablespoon chili powder

3 cloves garlic, minced, divided

2 teaspoons paprika

1½ teaspoons ground red pepper

1¼ teaspoons black pepper, divided

1 teaspoon onion powder

2 top sirloin steaks (about 8 ounces each, 1 inch thick)

3 tablespoons butter, divided

1 tablespoon olive oil

1 large onion, thinly sliced

8 ounces sliced mushrooms (white and shiitake or all white)

¼ teaspoon plus ⅛ teaspoon salt, divided

1 Combine water, Worcestershire sauce, soy sauce, chili powder, 2 cloves garlic, paprika, red pepper, 1 teaspoon black pepper and onion powder in small bowl; mix well. Place steaks in large resealable food storage bag; pour marinade over steaks. Seal bag; turn to coat. Marinate in refrigerator 1 to 3 hours.

2 Remove steaks from marinade 30 minutes before cooking; discard marinade and pat steaks dry with paper towel. Prepare grill for direct cooking. Oil grid.

3 While grill is preheating, heat 1 tablespoon butter and oil in large skillet over medium-high heat. Add onion; cook 5 minutes, stirring occasionally. Add mushrooms, ¼ teaspoon salt and remaining ¼ teaspoon black pepper; cook 10 minutes or until onion is golden brown and mushrooms begin to brown, stirring occasionally.

4 Combine remaining 2 tablespoons butter, 1 clove garlic and ⅛ teaspoon salt in small skillet; cook over medium-low heat 3 minutes or until garlic begins to sizzle.

5 Grill steaks over medium-high heat 6 minutes; turn and grill 6 minutes for medium rare or until desired doneness. Brush both sides of steaks with garlic butter during last 2 minutes of cooking. Remove to plate and tent with foil; let rest 5 minutes. Serve steaks with onion and mushroom mixture.

CHICKEN SCALOPPINE WITH MUSHROOMS AND ARTICHOKES

MAKES 4 SERVINGS

½ cup all-purpose flour

½ teaspoon salt

¼ teaspoon black pepper

4 boneless skinless chicken breasts (about 6 ounces each)

5 tablespoons butter, divided

2 tablespoons olive oil, divided

1 package (3 to 4 ounces) diced pancetta *or* ⅓ cup diced prosciutto

1 pound sliced mushrooms

1 can (14 ounces) artichoke hearts, sliced

3 tablespoons capers, rinsed and drained

⅓ cup lemon juice

3 tablespoons dry white wine

¾ cup whipping cream

2 teaspoons cornstarch

¾ cup chicken broth

Additional black pepper

1 package (16 ounces) angel hair pasta, cooked and drained

Chopped fresh parsley (optional)

1 Preheat oven to 250°F. Line baking sheet with foil. Combine flour, ½ teaspoon salt and ¼ teaspoon pepper in shallow dish. Pound chicken to ⅛-inch thickness between sheets of waxed paper with meat mallet or rolling pin. Cut each chicken breast in half crosswise. Coat both sides of chicken with flour mixture, shaking off excess.

2 Heat 1 tablespoon butter and 1 tablespoon oil in large skillet over medium-high heat. Add chicken in single layer; cook about 3 minutes per side or until golden brown. (Cook chicken in batches if necessary.) Remove to prepared baking sheet; place in oven to keep warm.

3 Add pancetta to skillet; cook and stir over medium heat 3 minutes or until lightly browned, scraping up browned bits from bottom of skillet. Add mushrooms; cook about 8 minutes or until mushrooms begin to brown, stirring occasionally. (Add additional 1 tablespoon oil if necessary to cook mushrooms.) Stir in artichokes and capers; cook 4 minutes. Reduce heat to low while preparing sauce.

4 Combine lemon juice and wine in small saucepan; bring to a boil over medium-high heat. Boil until reduced by one third. Stir in cream; cook over medium heat 4 minutes or until slightly thickened. Stir cornstarch into broth in small bowl until blended. Add to saucepan; cook and stir 3 minutes or until sauce thickens. Add remaining 4 tablespoons butter, 1 tablespoon at a time, whisking until sauce is smooth and well blended. Add sauce to mushroom mixture; cook and stir until heated through. Season with additional pepper.

5 Divide pasta among 4 plates; top with mushroom mixture and chicken. Garnish with parsley.

COCONUT SHRIMP

MAKES 4 SERVINGS

DIPPING SAUCE

- ½ cup orange marmalade
- ⅓ cup Thai chili sauce
- 1 teaspoon prepared horseradish
- ½ teaspoon salt

SHRIMP

- 1 cup flat beer
- 1 cup all-purpose flour
- 2 cups sweetened flaked coconut, divided
- 2 tablespoons sugar
- Vegetable oil for frying
- 16 to 20 large raw shrimp, peeled and deveined (with tails on), patted dry

1 For sauce, combine marmalade, chili sauce, horseradish and salt in small bowl; mix well. Cover and refrigerate until ready to serve.

2 For shrimp, whisk beer, flour, ½ cup coconut and sugar in large bowl until well blended. Refrigerate batter until oil is hot. Place remaining 1½ cups coconut in medium bowl.

3 Heat 2 inches of oil in large saucepan over medium heat to 350°F; adjust heat to maintain temperature. Dip each shrimp in beer batter, then in coconut, turning to coat completely. Cook shrimp, 4 at a time, 2 to 3 minutes or until golden brown, turning halfway through cooking time. Drain on paper towel-lined plate. Serve immediately with dipping sauce.

MEATLOAF

MAKES 4 TO 6 SERVINGS

1 tablespoon vegetable oil

2 green onions, minced

¼ cup minced green bell pepper

¼ cup grated carrot

3 cloves garlic, minced

¾ cup milk

2 eggs, beaten

1 pound ground beef

1 pound ground pork

1 cup plain dry bread crumbs

2 teaspoons salt

½ teaspoon onion powder

½ teaspoon black pepper

½ cup ketchup, divided

1 Preheat oven to 350°F.

2 Heat oil in large skillet over medium-high heat. Add green onions, bell pepper, carrot and garlic; cook and stir about 5 minutes or until vegetables are softened.

3 Whisk milk and eggs in medium bowl until well blended. Gently mix beef, pork, bread crumbs, salt, onion powder and black pepper in large bowl with hands. Add milk mixture, vegetables and ¼ cup ketchup; mix gently. Press into 9×5-inch loaf pan; place pan on rimmed baking sheet.

4 Bake 30 minutes. Spread remaining ¼ cup ketchup over meatloaf; bake 1 hour or until cooked through (165°F). Cool in pan 10 minutes; cut into slices.

MISO SALMON

MAKES 4 SERVINGS

1 cup uncooked long grain rice

4 salmon fillets (about 6 ounces each)

¼ cup packed brown sugar

¼ cup red or white miso

2 tablespoons soy sauce

1 tablespoon hot water

1 tablespoon butter

1 tablespoon minced fresh ginger

1 tablespoon minced shallot or red onion

½ cup plus 1 teaspoon sake, divided

1 tablespoon whipping cream or half-and-half

½ cup (1 stick) cold butter, cut into small pieces

1 teaspoon lime juice

½ teaspoon salt

2 green onions, julienned

1 Cook rice according to package directions; keep warm.

2 Preheat broiler. Spray 13×9-inch baking pan with nonstick cooking spray. Place salmon in prepared pan.

3 Whisk brown sugar, miso, soy sauce and hot water in small bowl until well blended. Spoon half of mixture evenly over salmon. Broil 10 minutes or until fish begins to flake when tested with fork, spooning remaining miso mixture over salmon twice during cooking.

4 Meanwhile, melt 1 tablespoon butter in small saucepan over medium heat. Add ginger and shallot; cook and stir 3 minutes or until softened. Add ½ cup sake; bring to a boil over medium-high heat. Cook 3 to 5 minutes or until reduced to 2 tablespoons. Whisk in cream. Add cold butter, one piece at a time, whisking constantly until butter is incorporated before adding next piece. Remove from heat; whisk in remaining 1 teaspoon sake, lime juice and ½ teaspoon salt. Season with additional salt, if desired.

5 Spread sauce on 4 plates; top with rice, salmon and green onions.

AUSSIE CHICKEN

MAKES 4 SERVINGS

½ cup honey

½ cup Dijon mustard

2 tablespoons vegetable oil, divided

1 teaspoon lemon juice

4 boneless skinless chicken breasts (about 1½ pounds)

Salt and black pepper

1 tablespoon butter

2 cups sliced mushrooms

4 slices bacon, cooked

½ cup (2 ounces) shredded Cheddar cheese

½ cup (2 ounces) shredded Monterey Jack cheese

Chopped fresh parsley

1 Whisk honey, mustard, 1 tablespoon oil and lemon juice in medium bowl until well blended. Remove half of marinade mixture to use as sauce; cover and refrigerate until ready to serve.

2 Place chicken in large resealable food storage bag. Pour remaining half of marinade over chicken; seal bag and turn to coat. Refrigerate at least 2 hours.

3 Preheat oven to 375°F. Remove chicken from marinade; discard marinade. Heat remaining 1 tablespoon oil in large ovenproof skillet over medium-high heat. Add chicken; cook 3 to 4 minutes per side or until golden brown. (Chicken will not be cooked through.) Remove chicken to plate; sprinkle with salt and pepper.

4 Heat butter in same skillet over medium-high heat. Add mushrooms; cook about 8 minutes or until mushrooms begin to brown, stirring occasionally and scraping up browned bits from bottom of skillet. Season with salt and pepper. Return chicken to skillet; spoon mushrooms over chicken. Top with bacon; sprinkle with Cheddar and Monterey Jack cheeses.

5 Bake 8 to 10 minutes or until chicken is no longer pink in center and cheese is melted. Sprinkle with parsley; serve with reserved honey mustard mixture.

STEAK FAJITAS

MAKES 2 SERVINGS

¼ cup lime juice

¼ cup soy sauce

4 tablespoons vegetable oil, divided

2 tablespoons honey

2 tablespoons Worcestershire sauce

2 cloves garlic, minced

½ teaspoon ground red pepper

1 pound flank steak, skirt steak or top sirloin

1 large yellow onion, halved and cut into ¼-inch slices

1 green bell pepper, cut into ¼-inch strips

1 red bell pepper, cut into ¼-inch strips

Flour tortillas, warmed

Lime wedges, pico de gallo, guacamole, sour cream, shredded lettuce and shredded Cheddar-Jack cheese (optional)

1 Combine lime juice, soy sauce, 2 tablespoons oil, honey, Worcestershire sauce, garlic and ground red pepper in medium bowl; mix well. Remove ¼ cup marinade to large bowl. Place steak in large resealable food storage bag. Pour remaining marinade over steak; seal bag and turn to coat. Marinate in refrigerator at least 2 hours or overnight. Add onion and bell peppers to bowl with ¼ cup marinade; toss to coat. Cover and refrigerate until ready to use.

2 Remove steak from marinade; discard marinade and wipe off excess from steak. Heat 1 tablespoon oil in large skillet (preferably cast iron) over medium-high heat. Cook steak about 4 minutes per side for medium rare or to desired doneness. Remove to cutting board; tent with foil and let rest 5 minutes.

3 Meanwhile, heat remaining 1 tablespoon oil in same skillet over medium-high heat. Add vegetable mixture; cook about 8 minutes or until vegetables are crisp-tender and beginning to brown in spots, stirring occasionally. (Cook in two batches if necessary.)

4 Cut steak into thin slices across the grain. Serve with vegetables, tortillas, lime wedges and desired toppings.

SIDE DISHES

CHEDDAR BISCUITS
MAKES 15 BISCUITS

2 cups all-purpose flour

1 tablespoon sugar

1 tablespoon baking powder

2¼ teaspoons garlic powder, divided

¾ teaspoon plus pinch of salt, divided

1 cup whole milk

½ cup (1 stick) plus 3 tablespoons butter, melted, divided

2 cups (8 ounces) shredded Cheddar cheese

½ teaspoon dried parsley flakes

1 Preheat oven to 450°F. Line large baking sheet with parchment paper.

2 Combine flour, sugar, baking powder, 2 teaspoons garlic powder and ¾ teaspoon salt in large bowl; mix well. Add milk and ½ cup melted butter; stir just until dry ingredients are moistened. Stir in cheese just until blended. Drop scant ¼ cupfuls of dough about 1½ inches apart onto prepared baking sheet.

3 Bake 10 to 12 minutes or until golden brown. Meanwhile, combine remaining 3 tablespoons melted butter, ¼ teaspoon garlic powder, pinch of salt and parsley flakes in small bowl; brush over biscuits immediately after removing from oven. Serve warm.

SMASHED POTATOES
MAKES 4 SERVINGS

4 medium russet potatoes
(about 1½ pounds), peeled
and cut into ¼-inch cubes

⅓ cup milk

2 tablespoons sour cream

1 tablespoon minced onion

½ teaspoon salt

¼ teaspoon black pepper

⅛ teaspoon garlic powder
(optional)

Chopped fresh chives or French
fried onions (optional)

1 Bring large saucepan of lightly salted water to a boil. Add potatoes; cook 15 to
20 minutes or until fork-tender. Drain and return to saucepan.

2 Slightly mash potatoes. Stir in milk, sour cream, minced onion, salt, pepper and
garlic powder, if desired. Mash until desired texture is reached, leaving potatoes
chunky. Cook about 5 minutes over low heat until heated through, stirring
occasionally. Top with chives, if desired.

SOFT GARLIC BREADSTICKS

MAKES ABOUT 16 BREADSTICKS

1½ cups water

6 tablespoons (¾ stick) butter, divided

4 cups all-purpose flour

2 tablespoons sugar

1 package (¼ ounce) active dry yeast

1½ teaspoons salt

¾ teaspoon coarse salt

¼ teaspoon garlic powder

1 Heat water and 2 tablespoons butter in small saucepan or microwavable bowl to 110° to 115°F. (Butter does not need to melt completely.)

2 Combine flour, sugar, yeast and 1½ teaspoons salt in large bowl of stand mixer; beat at low speed to combine. Add water mixture; beat until dough begins to come together. Knead at low speed with dough hook about 5 minutes or until dough is smooth and elastic. Shape dough into a ball. Place in large greased bowl; turn to grease top. Cover and let rise in warm place about 1 hour or until doubled in size.

3 Line two baking sheets with parchment paper or spray with nonstick cooking spray. Punch down dough. For each breadstick, pull off piece of dough slightly larger than a golf ball (about 2 ounces) and roll between hands or on work surface into 7-inch-long stick. Place on prepared baking sheets; cover loosely and let rise in warm place about 45 minutes or until doubled in size.

4 Preheat oven to 400°F. Melt remaining 4 tablespoons butter in small bowl. Brush breadsticks with 2 tablespoons butter; sprinkle with coarse salt.

5 Bake breadsticks 13 to 15 minutes or until golden brown. Stir garlic powder into remaining 2 tablespoons melted butter; brush over breadsticks immediately after removing from oven. Serve warm.

SIMPLE GOLDEN CORNBREAD

MAKES 9 TO 12 SERVINGS

1¼ cups all-purpose flour

¾ cup yellow cornmeal

⅓ cup sugar

2 teaspoons baking powder

1 teaspoon salt

1¼ cups whole milk

¼ cup (½ stick) butter, melted

1 egg

Honey Butter (recipe follows, optional)

1 Preheat oven to 400°F. Spray 8-inch square baking dish or pan with nonstick cooking spray.

2 Combine flour, cornmeal, sugar, baking powder and salt in large bowl; mix well. Beat milk, butter and egg in medium bowl until well blended. Add to flour mixture; stir just until dry ingredients are moistened. Pour batter into prepared baking dish.

3 Bake about 25 minutes or until golden brown and toothpick inserted into center comes out clean. Prepare Honey Butter, if desired. Serve with cornbread.

HONEY BUTTER

Beat 6 tablespoons (¾ stick) softened butter and ¼ cup honey in medium bowl with electric mixer at medium-high speed until light and creamy.

COLESLAW

MAKES 10 SERVINGS

1 medium head green cabbage, shredded

1 medium carrot, shredded

½ cup mayonnaise

½ cup milk

⅓ cup sugar

3 tablespoons lemon juice

1½ tablespoons white vinegar

½ teaspoon salt

⅛ teaspoon black pepper

1 Combine cabbage and carrot in large bowl; mix well.

2 Combine mayonnaise, milk, sugar, lemon juice, vinegar, salt and pepper in medium bowl; whisk until well blended. Add to cabbage mixture; stir until blended.

HUSH PUPPIES
MAKES ABOUT 24 HUSH PUPPIES

1½ cups yellow cornmeal

½ cup all-purpose flour

2 teaspoons baking powder

¾ teaspoon salt

1 cup milk

1 small onion, minced

1 egg, lightly beaten

Vegetable oil

1 Combine cornmeal, flour, baking powder and salt in medium bowl; mix well. Add milk, onion and egg; stir until well blended. Let batter stand 5 to 10 minutes.

2 Heat 1 inch of oil in large heavy skillet over medium-high heat to 375°F; adjust heat to maintain temperature. Drop batter by tablespoonfuls into hot oil. Cook, in batches, 2 minutes or until golden brown. Drain on paper towel-lined plate. Serve warm.

CLASSIC MACARONI AND CHEESE

MAKES 8 SERVINGS

2 cups uncooked elbow macaroni pasta

¼ cup (½ stick) butter

¼ cup all-purpose flour

2½ cups whole milk

1 teaspoon salt

⅛ teaspoon black pepper

4 cups (16 ounces) shredded Colby Jack cheese

1 Cook pasta according to package directions until al dente; drain.

2 Melt butter in large saucepan over medium heat. Add flour; whisk until well blended and bubbly. Gradually add milk, salt and pepper, whisking until blended. Cook and stir until milk begins to bubble. Add cheese, 1 cup at a time; cook and stir until cheese is melted and sauce is smooth.

3 Add cooked pasta; stir gently until blended. Cook until heated through.

SIDE DISHES

CHEESY GARLIC BREAD

MAKES 8 TO 10 SERVINGS

1 loaf (about 16 ounces) Italian bread

½ cup (1 stick) butter, softened

8 cloves garlic, very thinly sliced

¼ cup grated Parmesan cheese

2 cups (8 ounces) shredded mozzarella cheese

1 Preheat oven to 425°F. Line large baking sheet with foil.

2 Cut bread in half horizontally. Spread cut sides of bread evenly with butter; top with sliced garlic. Sprinkle with Parmesan, then mozzarella cheeses. Place on prepared baking sheet.

3 Bake about 12 minutes or until cheeses are melted and golden brown in spots. Cut crosswise into slices. Serve warm.

DESSERTS

CHOCOLATE CHUNK PIZZA COOKIE
MAKES 3 PIZZA COOKIES (2 TO 3 SERVINGS EACH)

2 cups all-purpose flour

1 teaspoon baking soda

1 teaspoon salt

¾ cup (1½ sticks) butter, softened

1 cup packed brown sugar

¼ cup granulated sugar

2 eggs

1 teaspoon vanilla

1 package (about 11 ounces) chocolate chunks

Vanilla ice cream

1 Preheat oven to 400°F. Spray 3 (6-inch) cast iron skillets, cake pans or deep-dish pizza pans with nonstick cooking spray.*

2 Combine flour, baking soda and salt in medium bowl. Beat butter, brown sugar and granulated sugar in large bowl with electric mixer at medium speed until creamy. Beat in eggs and vanilla until well blended. Gradually beat in flour mixture at low speed just until blended. Stir in chocolate chunks. Spread dough evenly in prepared pans.

3 Bake about 15 minutes or until top and edges are deep golden brown but center is still slightly soft. Top with ice cream. Serve warm.

If you don't have 3 skillets or pans, you can bake one at a time. Refrigerate the cookie dough between batches, and make sure the skillet is completely cool before adding more dough. (Clean and spray the skillet again with each new batch.)

WARM APPLE CROSTATA

MAKES 4 TARTS (4 TO 8 SERVINGS)

1¾ cups all-purpose flour

⅓ cup granulated sugar

½ teaspoon plus ⅛ teaspoon salt, divided

¾ cup (1½ sticks) cold butter, cut into pieces

3 tablespoons ice water

2 teaspoons vanilla

8 Pink Lady or Honeycrisp apples (about 1½ pounds), peeled and cut into ¼-inch slices

¼ cup packed brown sugar

1 tablespoon lemon juice

1 teaspoon ground cinnamon

⅛ teaspoon ground nutmeg

4 teaspoons butter, cut into very small pieces

1 egg, beaten

1 to 2 teaspoons coarse sugar

Vanilla ice cream

Caramel sauce or ice cream topping

1 Combine flour, ⅓ cup granulated sugar and ½ teaspoon salt in food processor; process 5 seconds. Add ¾ cup butter; process about 10 seconds or until mixture resembles coarse crumbs.

2 Combine ice water and vanilla in small bowl. With motor running, pour mixture through feed tube; process 12 seconds or until dough begins to come together. Shape dough into a disc; wrap in plastic wrap and refrigerate 30 minutes.

3 Meanwhile, combine apples, brown sugar, lemon juice, cinnamon, nutmeg and remaining ⅛ teaspoon salt in large bowl; toss to coat. Preheat oven to 400°F.

4 Line 2 baking sheets with parchment paper. Cut dough into 4 pieces; roll out each piece into 7-inch circle on floured surface. Place circles on prepared baking sheets; mound apples in center of dough circles (about 1 cup apples for each crostata). Fold or roll up edges of dough towards center to create rim of crostata. Dot apples with remaining 4 teaspoons butter. Brush dough with egg; sprinkle dough and apples with coarse sugar.

5 Bake about 20 minutes or until apples are tender and crust is golden brown. Serve warm topped with ice cream and caramel sauce.

TURTLE CHEESECAKE

MAKES 12 SERVINGS

CRUST

½ cup (1 stick) butter

4 ounces semisweet baking chocolate, chopped

½ cup sugar

2 eggs

½ teaspoon salt

½ teaspoon vanilla

¾ cup all-purpose flour

½ cup finely chopped pecans

FILLING

4 packages (8 ounces each) cream cheese, softened

1 cup sugar

1½ teaspoons vanilla

½ cup sour cream

4 eggs

½ cup caramel topping

TOPPING

½ cup chopped pecans

2 tablespoons caramel topping

GARNISH

1 cup prepared fudge frosting

1 Preheat oven to 350°F. Spray 9-inch springform pan with nonstick cooking spray. Wrap outside of pan with foil.

2 For crust, melt butter and chocolate in medium saucepan over low heat, stirring frequently until smooth. Remove from heat; stir in ½ cup sugar until blended. Add 2 eggs, one at a time, stirring until well blended after each addition. Stir in salt and ½ teaspoon vanilla. Stir in flour and ½ cup pecans just until blended. Spread evenly in prepared pan. Bake 15 minutes or until top is set but still soft. Remove from oven and place in larger baking pan.

3 For filling, beat cream cheese in large bowl with electric mixer at low speed until creamy. Add 1 cup sugar and 1½ teaspoons vanilla; beat until well blended. Add sour cream; beat until blended. With mixer running at medium speed, add 4 eggs, one at a time, beating until well blended after each addition. Spread half of filling over crust. Drop ¼ cup caramel topping by teaspoonfuls over filling; swirl with skewer or knife. Top with remaining filling. Drop remaining ¼ cup caramel topping by teaspoonfuls over filling; swirl with skewer. Place pan in oven; add hot water to larger pan to come halfway up side of springform pan.

4 Bake 1 hour or until top of cheesecake is almost set. Immediately run knife around side of cheesecake to loosen. Cool completely in pan on wire rack. Refrigerate 4 hours or overnight.

5 For topping, cook and stir ½ cup pecans in small skillet over medium-low heat 3 to 5 minutes or until fragrant and lightly browned. Add 2 tablespoons caramel topping; cook and stir 1 minute or until nuts are glazed. Spread over cheesecake.

6 Place frosting in piping bag or large resealable food storage bag fitted with large star tip. Pipe rosettes around edge of cheesecake.

KEY LIME PIE
MAKES 8 SERVINGS

12 whole graham crackers*

⅓ cup butter, melted

3 tablespoons sugar

2 cans (14 ounces each) sweetened condensed milk

¾ cup key lime juice

6 egg yolks

Pinch of salt

Whipped cream (optional)

Lime slices (optional)

*Or substitute 1½ cups graham cracker crumbs.

1 Preheat oven to 350°F. Spray 9-inch pie plate or springform pan with nonstick cooking spray.

2 Place graham crackers in food processor; pulse until coarse crumbs form. Add butter and sugar; pulse until well blended. Press mixture onto bottom and 1 inch up side of prepared pie plate. Bake 8 minutes or until lightly browned. Remove to wire rack to cool 10 minutes. *Reduce oven temperature to 325°F.*

3 Meanwhile, beat sweetened condensed milk, lime juice, egg yolks and salt in large bowl with electric mixer at medium-low speed 1 minute or until well blended and smooth. Pour into crust.

4 Bake 20 minutes or until top is set. Cool completely in pan on wire rack. Cover and refrigerate 2 hours or overnight. Garnish with whipped cream and lime slices.

DESSERTS

CHOCOLATE STORM

MAKES 9 SERVINGS

12 ounces semisweet chocolate, chopped

12 ounces bittersweet chocolate, chopped

¾ cup (1½ sticks) butter

5 eggs

⅔ cup granulated sugar

2 teaspoons vanilla

½ teaspoon salt

1¼ cups chopped pecans

2 cups cold whipping cream

¼ cup powdered sugar

3 pints vanilla ice cream

1½ cups hot fudge topping, heated

Chocolate curls (optional)

1 Preheat oven to 325°F. Spray 9-inch square baking pan with nonstick cooking spray.

2 Combine semisweet chocolate, bittersweet chocolate and butter in medium microwavable bowl. Microwave on HIGH 1 minute; stir and repeat. Microwave 30 seconds; stir until chocolate is melted and mixture is smooth.

3 Beat eggs, granulated sugar, vanilla and salt in large bowl with electric mixer at medium speed 1 minute. Beat at high speed 1 minute. Add half of chocolate mixture; beat at low speed until blended. Beat in remaining chocolate mixture until blended. Stir in pecans. Pour batter into prepared pan, spreading to make top level and smooth.

4 Bake about 45 minutes or until center of brownie begins to firm. Cool in pan on wire rack.*

5 When ready to serve, beat cream and powdered sugar in medium bowl with electric mixer at medium-high speed until stiff peaks form. Cut brownie into 9 squares. If desired, heat individual brownie squares in microwave on HIGH 30 seconds. Top each brownie with scoop of ice cream; drizzle with hot fudge. Top with whipped cream and chocolate curls, if desired.

Brownie can be served soon after baking but is more difficult to cut when warm.

INTENSE LEMON CAKE

MAKES 9 TO 12 SERVINGS

CAKE

1¾ cups all-purpose flour

1¼ teaspoons baking powder

½ teaspoon salt

4 eggs, separated

1½ cups granulated sugar

¾ cup (1½ sticks) butter, softened

Grated peel of 2 lemons
(1 tablespoon)

¼ cup lemon juice

LEMON CURD

1 cup granulated sugar

¾ cup (1½ sticks) butter

⅔ cup lemon juice

Grated peel of 2 lemons
(1 tablespoon)

¼ teaspoon salt

5 eggs, beaten

¼ cup whipping cream

TOPPING

1 package (8 ounces)
cream cheese, softened

1½ cups powdered sugar

Lemon peel strips (optional)

1 Preheat oven to 350°F. Spray 9-inch square baking pan with nonstick cooking spray.

2 For cake, combine flour, baking powder and ½ teaspoon salt in medium bowl. Beat 4 egg whites in large bowl with electric mixer until stiff peaks form. Transfer to small bowl.

3 Beat 1½ cups granulated sugar and ¾ cup butter in large bowl with electric mixer at medium speed until light and fluffy. Add 4 egg yolks, one at a time, beating well after each addition. Add 1 tablespoon lemon peel and ¼ cup lemon juice; beat until well blended. Beat in flour mixture at low speed just until blended. Gently stir in half of egg whites. Fold in remaining egg whites until no streaks of white remain. Spread batter in prepared pan.

4 Bake 35 to 38 minutes or until toothpick inserted into center comes out clean. Cool in pan on wire rack 10 minutes.

5 Meanwhile, for lemon curd, combine 1 cup granulated sugar, ¾ cup butter, ⅔ cup lemon juice, 1 tablespoon lemon peel and ¼ teaspoon salt in medium saucepan; cook over medium heat until butter is melted and sugar is dissolved, stirring frequently. Gradually whisk in beaten eggs in thin, steady stream. Cook over medium-low heat 5 minutes or until thickened to consistency of pudding, whisking constantly.

Strain through fine-mesh sieve into medium bowl. Remove ½ cup lemon curd to small bowl. Press plastic wrap onto surface of remaining lemon curd; cool to room temperature. Refrigerate until cold and thickened.

6 Stir cream into reserved ½ cup lemon curd. Poke holes all over warm cake with skewer. Pour cream mixture over cake, spreading to cover surface and pressing mixture into holes. Cover and refrigerate 1 hour.

7 For topping, beat cream cheese in large bowl with electric mixer at medium speed 1 minute or until creamy. Add powdered sugar and 1 cup lemon curd; beat 2 minutes or until well blended and fluffy. Spread remaining lemon curd over top of cake. Gently spread topping over lemon curd layer. Refrigerate 2 hours or overnight. Garnish with lemon peel strips.

TIRAMISU

MAKES 9 SERVINGS

¾ cup sugar

4 egg yolks

1 cup plus 2 tablespoons whipping cream, divided

16 ounces mascarpone cheese

½ teaspoon vanilla

¾ cup cold strong brewed coffee

¼ cup coffee-flavored liqueur

24 to 28 ladyfingers

2 teaspoons unsweetened cocoa powder

1 Fill medium saucepan half full with water; bring to a boil over high heat. Reduce heat to low to maintain a simmer. Whisk sugar, egg yolks and 2 tablespoons cream in medium metal bowl until well blended. Place over simmering water; cook 6 to 8 minutes or until thickened, whisking constantly. Remove from heat; cool slightly. Whisk in mascarpone and vanilla until smooth and well blended.

2 Pour remaining 1 cup cream into bowl of electric mixer; beat at high speed until stiff peaks form. Gently fold whipped cream into mascarpone mixture until no streaks of white remain.

3 Combine coffee and liqueur in shallow bowl; mix well. Working with one at a time, dip ladyfingers briefly in coffee mixture; arrange in single layer in 9-inch square baking pan, trimming cookies to fit as necessary. Spread thin layer of custard over ladyfingers, covering completely. Dip remaining ladyfingers in remaining coffee mixture; arrange in single layer over custard. Spread remaining custard over cookies. Place cocoa in fine-mesh strainer; sprinkle over custard. Refrigerate 2 hours or overnight.

MOLTEN CHOCOLATE CAKES
MAKES 8 CAKES

1 package (about 15 ounces) chocolate fudge cake mix

1½ cups water

3 eggs

½ cup canola or vegetable oil

4 ounces bittersweet chocolate, chopped

4 ounces semisweet chocolate, chopped

½ cup whipping cream

¼ cup (½ stick) butter, cut into pieces

1 tablespoon light corn syrup

¼ teaspoon vanilla

⅛ teaspoon salt

Caramel topping

Vanilla ice cream

1 Preheat oven to 350°F. Spray 8 jumbo (3½-inch) muffin cups with nonstick cooking spray.

2 Beat cake mix, water, eggs and oil in large bowl with electric mixer at low speed 30 seconds. Beat at medium speed 2 minutes. Pour ½ cup batter into each prepared muffin cup; discard remaining batter. Bake about 25 minutes or until toothpick inserted into centers comes out clean. Cool in pan 5 minutes; remove to wire racks to cool.

3 Meanwhile, combine bittersweet chocolate, semisweet chocolate, cream, butter, corn syrup, vanilla and salt in medium microwavable bowl; microwave on HIGH 30 seconds. Stir; microwave at additional 30-second intervals until chocolate begins to melt. Whisk until smooth. Reserve ½ cup chocolate mixture in small microwavable bowl for topping.

4 When cakes have cooled, cut off domed top of each cake with serrated knife. Invert cakes so wider part is on the bottom. Use 1½-inch biscuit cutter or small serrated knife to remove hole in top of each cake (narrow part) about 1 inch deep. Reserve cake from holes for serving.

5 Fill hole in each cake with 2 tablespoons chocolate mixture; top with reserved cake pieces. Microwave reserved ½ cup chocolate mixture on HIGH 20 seconds or until melted.

6 For each serving, drizzle caramel topping on microwavable plate. Arrange cake on plate; microwave on HIGH about 30 seconds until chocolate filling is hot. Top with ice cream; drizzle with warm chocolate mixture.

BANANA CREAM PIE
MAKES 8 SERVINGS

1 refrigerated pie crust
    (half of 15-ounce package),
    at room temperature

⅔ cup sugar

¼ cup cornstarch

¼ teaspoon salt

2½ cups milk

4 egg yolks, beaten

2 tablespoons butter, softened

2 teaspoons vanilla

2 medium bananas

1 teaspoon lemon juice

Whipped cream and toasted
    sliced almonds*

*To toast almonds, spread on baking
sheet. Bake in preheated 350°F oven
6 to 8 minutes or until golden brown,
stirring frequently.

1 Preheat oven to 400°F. Line 9-inch pie plate with crust; flute edge. Prick bottom and side all over with fork. Bake 10 minutes or until crust is golden brown. Cool completely.

2 Combine sugar, cornstarch and salt in medium saucepan. Whisk in milk until well blended. Cook over medium heat about 12 minutes or until mixture boils and thickens, stirring constantly. Boil 2 minutes, stirring constantly. Remove from heat.

3 Gradually whisk ½ hot cup milk mixture into egg yolks in small bowl. Gradually whisk mixture back into milk mixture in saucepan. Cook over medium heat about 5 minutes, whisking constantly. Remove from heat; whisk in butter and vanilla. Cool 20 minutes, stirring occasionally. Strain through fine-mesh strainer into medium bowl. Press plastic wrap onto surface of pudding; cool about 30 minutes or until lukewarm.

4 Cut bananas into ¼-inch slices; toss with lemon juice in medium bowl. Spread half of pudding in cooled crust; arrange bananas over pudding. (Reserve several banana slices for garnish, if desired.) Spread remaining pudding over bananas. Refrigerate 4 hours or overnight. Garnish with whipped cream, almonds and reserved banana slices.

STRAWBERRY CHEESECAKE DESSERT SHOOTERS

MAKES 8 TO 10 SERVINGS

1 cup graham cracker crumbs, plus additional for garnish

¼ cup (½ stick) butter, melted

2 cups chopped fresh strawberries

¾ cup sugar, divided

12 ounces cream cheese, softened

2 eggs

2 tablespoons sour cream

½ teaspoon vanilla

Whipped cream

1 Place 1 cup graham cracker crumbs in medium nonstick skillet; cook and stir over medium heat about 3 minutes or until lightly browned. Transfer to small bowl; stir in butter until well blended. Press mixture evenly into 8 to 10 (3- to 4-ounce) shot glasses.*

2 Combine strawberries and ¼ cup sugar in medium bowl; toss to coat. Cover and refrigerate until ready to serve.

3 Beat cream cheese in medium bowl with electric mixer at medium speed until creamy. Add eggs, remaining ½ cup sugar, sour cream and vanilla; beat until well blended. Transfer to medium saucepan; cook over medium heat 5 to 6 minutes or until thickened and smooth, stirring frequently. Divide filling evenly among prepared crusts. Refrigerate 1 hour or until cold.

4 Top each serving with strawberries and whipped cream. Garnish with additional graham cracker crumbs.

For larger servings, use 4 to 5 (6- to 8-ounce) juice or stemless wine glasses. Prepare as directed, dividing crumb mixture, filling and strawberries evenly among glasses.

CHOCOLATE OVERLOAD CAKE

MAKES 12 SERVINGS

4 cups all-purpose flour

4 cups sugar

1½ cups unsweetened cocoa powder

3½ teaspoons baking soda

1 tablespoon baking powder

2⅛ teaspoons salt, divided

4 eggs

2 cups buttermilk

1 cup vegetable or canola oil

4 teaspoons vanilla

2 cups very hot coffee

6¾ cups semisweet chocolate chips, divided

3 cups whipping cream

¼ cup light corn syrup

2 cups chopped walnuts

1 Preheat oven to 350°F. Spray bottoms of 3 (9-inch) round cake pans lightly with nonstick cooking spray; line with parchment paper. Spray bottoms and sides of pans with baking spray or grease and flour pans.

2 Combine flour, sugar, cocoa, baking soda, baking powder and 2 teaspoons salt in large bowl of electric mixer; mix well. Whisk eggs in medium bowl. Add buttermilk, oil and vanilla; whisk until well blended. Slowly add egg mixture to flour mixture (mixer will be very full), beating at low speed until blended. Beat at medium speed 2 minutes. Gradually add coffee, beating at low speed until blended. (Batter will be thin.) Pour batter into prepared pans. Sprinkle each layer with ¼ cup chocolate chips.

3 Bake about 45 minutes or until toothpick inserted into centers comes out clean. (Rotate cake pans from top to bottom and left to right halfway through baking.) Cool in pans 10 minutes; remove to wire racks to cool completely.

4 Combine cream, corn syrup and remaining ⅛ teaspoon salt in large microwavable bowl. Microwave on HIGH 4 minutes or just until mixture begins to bubble, stirring after each minute. Add remaining 6 cups chocolate chips; let stand 3 minutes. Whisk until well blended and smooth. Remove half of filling (about 4 cups) to medium bowl; refrigerate 30 minutes to 1 hour or until thick and spreadable. (Leave remaining mixture at room temperature for top and side of cake.)

5 Cut each cake layer in half horizontally with long serrated knife. Place one bottom cake layer, cut side up, on serving plate; spread with chilled filling (scant ⅔ cup per layer). Top with second top cake layer, cut side up; spread with filling. Repeat with remaining cake layers and chilled filling until final cake layer is reached; top layer should be placed cut side down over filling.

6 Microwave remaining chocolate mixture on LOW (30%) 2 to 3 minutes or just until pourable, stirring after each minute. Pour frosting over top of cake so it runs down side; use long metal spatula to smooth frosting around side of cake. Refrigerate 10 minutes or until frosting is partially set; gently press walnuts into side of cake.

CLASSIC FLAN

MAKES 6 SERVINGS

1½ cups sugar, divided

1 tablespoon water

¼ teaspoon ground cinnamon

3 cups whole milk

3 eggs

3 egg yolks

1 teaspoon vanilla

1 Preheat oven to 300°F.

2 Combine 1 cup sugar, water and cinnamon in medium saucepan; cook over medium-high heat without stirring about 10 minutes or until sugar is melted and mixture is deep golden amber in color. Pour into 6 (6-ounce) ramekins, swirling to coat bottoms. Place ramekins in 13×9-inch baking pan.

3 Heat milk in separate medium saucepan over medium heat until bubbles begin to form around edge of pan.

4 Meanwhile, whisk eggs, egg yolks, vanilla and remaining ½ cup sugar in medium bowl until well blended. Whisk in ½ cup hot milk in thin, steady stream. Gradually whisk in remaining milk. Divide milk mixture evenly among prepared ramekins. Carefully add hot water to larger baking pan until water comes halfway up sides of ramekins. Cover ramekins with waxed paper or parchment paper.

5 Bake 1 hour 15 minutes or until custard is firm and knife inserted into custard comes out clean. Remove ramekins from baking pan; cool completely. Cover and refrigerate until cold. Run small knife around edges of ramekins; unmold flan onto serving plates.

DESSERTS

RASPBERRY WHITE CHOCOLATE CHEESECAKE

MAKES 12 SERVINGS

24 crème-filled chocolate sandwich cookies, crushed into fine crumbs

3 tablespoons butter, melted

4 packages (8 ounces each) cream cheese, softened

1¼ cups sugar

½ cup sour cream

2 teaspoons vanilla

5 eggs, at room temperature

1 bar (4 ounces) white chocolate, chopped into ¼-inch pieces

¾ cup seedless raspberry jam, stirred

Shaved white chocolate

Whipped cream and fresh raspberries

1 Preheat oven to 350°F. Spray 9-inch springform pan with nonstick cooking spray. Line bottom and side of pan with parchment paper. Wrap outside of pan tightly with foil.

2 For crust, combine crushed cookies and butter in small bowl; mix well. Press mixture onto bottom and 1 inch up side of prepared pan. Bake about 8 minutes or until firm. Remove to wire rack to cool completely. *Increase oven temperature to 450°F.*

3 Beat cream cheese in large bowl with electric mixer at low speed until creamy. Add sugar, sour cream and vanilla; beat until smooth and well blended. Add eggs, one at a time, beating until blended after each addition. Fold in chopped white chocolate with spatula. Spread one third of filling in crust. Drop half of jam by teaspoonfuls over filling; swirl gently with small knife or skewer. Top with one third of filling; drop remaining half of jam by teaspoonfuls over filling and gently swirl jam. Spread remaining filling over top.

4 Place springform pan in larger baking pan; add hot water to larger pan to come halfway up side of springform pan. Carefully place in oven. *Immediately reduce oven temperature to 350°F.* Bake about 1 hour 10 minutes or until top of cheesecake is lightly browned and center jiggles slightly. Remove cheesecake from roasting pan to wire rack; remove foil. Cool to room temperature. Cover and refrigerate 4 hours or overnight. Garnish with shaved white chocolate, whipped cream and raspberries.

DESSERTS

RECIPE INDEX

RECIPE INDEX

RECIPE INDEX

TRADEMARKS

Applebee's is a registered trademark of Applebee's International, Ltd.

Bennigan's is a registered trademark of Bennigan's Grill & Tavern.

BJ's Restaurant & Brewhouse is a registered trademark of BJ's Restaurants, Inc.

Bonefish Grill is a registered trademark of Bonefish Grill, LLC.

Buca di Beppo is a registered trademark of Planet Hollywood International, Inc.

Buffalo Wild Wings is a registered trademark of Buffalo Wild Wings, Inc.

California Pizza Kitchen is a registered trademark of California Pizza Kitchen, Inc.

Carrabba's Italian Grill is a registered trademark of Bloomin' Brands, Inc.

Cheeseburger in Paradise is a registered trademark of Luby's Fuddruckers Restaurants, LLC.

The Cheesecake Factory is a registered trademark of The Cheesecake Factory, LLC.

Chevys Fresh Mex is a registered trademark of Chevys Inc.

Chick-fil-A is a registered trademark of CFA Properties, Inc.

Chili's is a registered trademark of Brinker International.

Chipotle Mexican Grill is a registered trademark of Chipotle Mexican Grill, Inc.

Cinnabon is a registered trademark of Cinnabon, Inc.

Claim Jumper is a registered trademark of Landry's, Inc.

Cracker Barrel is a registered trademark of CBOCS Properties, Inc.

Hard Rock Cafe is a registered trademark of Hard Rock Cafe International, Inc.

Houlihan's is a registered trademark of Houlihan's Restaurants, Inc.

IHOP is a registered trademark of International House of Pancakes, Inc.

Jason's deli is a registered trademark of DMI, Inc.

METRIC CONVERSION CHART

VOLUME MEASUREMENTS (dry)

1/8 teaspoon = 0.5 mL
1/4 teaspoon = 1 mL
1/2 teaspoon = 2 mL
3/4 teaspoon = 4 mL
1 teaspoon = 5 mL
1 tablespoon = 15 mL
2 tablespoons = 30 mL
1/4 cup = 60 mL
1/3 cup = 75 mL
1/2 cup = 125 mL
2/3 cup = 150 mL
3/4 cup = 175 mL
1 cup = 250 mL
2 cups = 1 pint = 500 mL
3 cups = 750 mL
4 cups = 1 quart = 1 L

VOLUME MEASUREMENTS (fluid)

1 fluid ounce (2 tablespoons) = 30 mL
4 fluid ounces (1/2 cup) = 125 mL
8 fluid ounces (1 cup) = 250 mL
12 fluid ounces (1 1/2 cups) = 375 mL
16 fluid ounces (2 cups) = 500 mL

WEIGHTS (mass)

1/2 ounce = 15 g
1 ounce = 30 g
3 ounces = 90 g
4 ounces = 120 g
8 ounces = 225 g
10 ounces = 285 g
12 ounces = 360 g
16 ounces = 1 pound = 450 g

DIMENSIONS

1/16 inch = 2 mm
1/8 inch = 3 mm
1/4 inch = 6 mm
1/2 inch = 1.5 cm
3/4 inch = 2 cm
1 inch = 2.5 cm

OVEN TEMPERATURES

250°F = 120°C
275°F = 140°C
300°F = 150°C
325°F = 160°C
350°F = 180°C
375°F = 190°C
400°F = 200°C
425°F = 220°C
450°F = 230°C

BAKING PAN SIZES

Utensil	Size in Inches/Quarts	Metric Volume	Size in Centimeters
Baking or Cake Pan (square or rectangular)	8×8×2	2 L	20×20×5
	9×9×2	2.5 L	23×23×5
	12×8×2	3 L	30×20×5
	13×9×2	3.5 L	33×23×5
Loaf Pan	8×4×3	1.5 L	20×10×7
	9×5×3	2 L	23×13×7
Round Layer Cake Pan	8×1½	1.2 L	20×4
	9×1½	1.5 L	23×4
Pie Plate	8×1¼	750 mL	20×3
	9×1¼	1 L	23×3
Baking Dish or Casserole	1 quart	1 L	—
	1½ quart	1.5 L	—
	2 quart	2 L	—